CUP TIED

STORIES AND SCENES FROM THE SCOTTISH CUP IN ITS 150TH YEAR

Photographs by Alan McCredie

Words by Daniel Gray

Cans, fags and makeshift stands. This architectural wonder stands in a back garden overlooking Camelon's Carmuirs Park.

HERE ARE CLUBS OF VINTAGE NICKNAMES – BLEACHERS AND BELTERS, LOONS AND MIGHTY MARINERS – PLAYING AT GROUNDS GLOWING WITH HOMESPUN CHARACTER AND CHARACTERS...

Roaring on from the sidelines at Camelon's Carmuirs Park.

...THIS IS FOOTBALL AS SEEN FROM THE GRASS MOUND AND THE TUMBLEDOWN TERRACE. THESE ARE THE PLACES WHERE TEENAGE ULTRAS BOUNCE AND OLD BOYS WARN THEM THEY'LL "GIE THEMSELVES GRUMPY KNEES"...

Cappie the Cat, the Greenock Morton mascot, chats to young fans before the fifth round tie against Motherwell.

…AN ELEGANT VOYAGE AMONG GIANTKILLERS AND CUP RUNS AND WEEKEND PLANS SPARKED BY THE WORDS: "AND THAT CONCLUDES THE DRAW…"

CONTENTS

10 INTRODUCTION
Ties will be played...
Like all cup runs, ours starts with the clack of numbered balls. Fixtures are conjured and travel plans sparked by the words 'And that concludes the draw.'

14 CHAPTER 1
Village people
And so it begins... Over two late Summer weekends, 55 teams plucked from across the land joust to make the First Round proper. Our journey starts beneath a village viaduct.

32 CHAPTER 2
Dreaming by the old canal
Autumn drifts in and makes our game look golden as Highland and Lowland League clubs join the shindig. For our next stop, we moor up near Falkirk.

50 CHAPTER 3
Mussel museum
With the changing of the clocks arrive chilly evenings perfect for floodlit dreaming. In the Lothians we find unexpected goals aplenty...

68 CHAPTER 4
Toonlight Serenade
Teams from the Championship and League One clock on, though 13 non-league sides remain. To the bright side of Fife we go for a floodlit Friday, and then north to see some fishermen's blues.

86 CHAPTER 5
Buckie bring the tonic
Our cup hibernated over Christmas and awoke in deepest winter. It was time for minnows to supply the light...

102 CHAPTER 6
Friday I'm in love
In two grand old theatres of football – Cappielow and Pittodrie – we greedily chased more underdog stories.

118 CHAPTER 7
North Sea blues
As western teams travelled eastwards to coastal homes, only eight clubs remained. Daydreams of past glories inspired hopes of May delight.

144 CHAPTER 8
The Hampden four
On an April weekend, troubled Dons and buoyant Jambos trek to Hampden. Greens and Blues await them, determined to concoct a first Old Firm final in two decades.

162 CHAPTER 9
And then there were two
Over the cup's course, 131 teams had been whittled to two. Now this famous pair restoked their rivalry at Hampden, marking the end of our odyssey.

182 CHAPTER 10
Something in the air
Finals of the Scottish Cup have been played at nine different venues. Here, aerial shots of those existent and demolished give a unique perspective.

190 THE RESULTS
The road from Hamlet to Hampden
131 teams took part, starting on 12 August 2023 and ending at Hampden Park on 25 May 2024.

Golden autumn makes Camelon Juniors' Carmuirs Park an idyllic place to watch football. Photograph by Daniel Gray

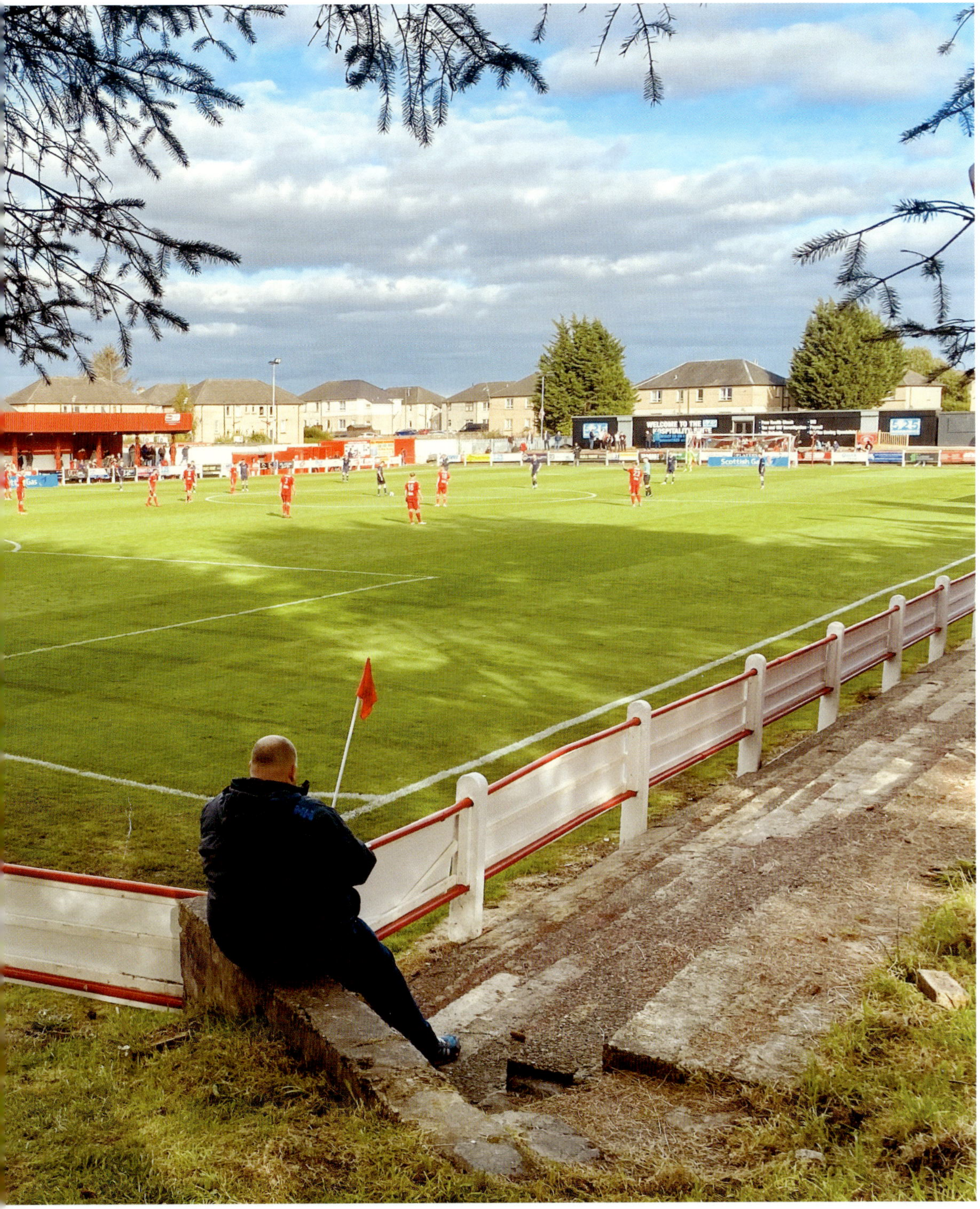

CUP TIED

Scenes and stories from the Scottish Cup in its 150th year

First published in Great Britain in 2024
This edition published 2024 by
BackPage & Nutmeg
www.backpagepress.co.uk
www.nutmegmagazine.co.uk

Copyright © The Scottish Football Association
ISBN: 9781909430624

The right of The Scottish Football Association to be identified as the author of this work has been asserted in accordance with the Copyright, Designs and Patents Act 1988. All rights reserved. No part of this publication may be reproduced, stored or transmitted in any form, or by any means electronic, mechanical, photocopying, recording or otherwise, without the express written permission of the publisher. A catalogue record for this book is available on request from the British Library.

Designed and typeset by
Ally Palmer, Nutmeg Media Ltd
Front cover image: Alan McCredie
Printed in Great Britain by Bell & Bain Ltd

Typeset by Nutmeg
Typography: Body text is Acta Roman
By Dino Dos Santos, DSType Foundry. www.dstype.com
Main headlines are Flama Ultra Condensed Black
By Mario Feliciano. www.felicianotypefoundry.com

The Scottish Cup trophy, the world's oldest in association football, sits outside the Hampden Bowling Club Pavilion on the site of the original Hampden Park where the trophy was first lifted by Queen's Park in 1874.

INTRODUCTION

TIES WILL BE PLAYED...

Like all cup runs, ours starts with the clack of numbered balls. Fixtures are conjured and travel plans sparked by the words "And that concludes the draw."

It is a cherished bowling club like so many hundreds of others. Varnished wooden panels hold oak boards that are embossed with the names of a century and more's champion players. On a cork noticeboard, sheets of paper request players for a friendly in Cambus (mixed, away), the Stan Eadie Open Mixed Triples at Giffnock (fee inclusive of filled roll on arrival) and the Tuesday afternoon Cathcart Seniors tournament. 'Liz Stark – Little Gem, 50s/60s singer' advertises her availability on a handwritten scrap of paper, just above two funeral orders of service for recently departed club members. Unlike a football changing room's medicant stench, the locker room hosts a sentimental aroma of Brylcreem and Digestive biscuits as if a scented candle named 'Traditional Grandad' is being burned.

Yet this clubhouse is like no other, for it occupies sacred land. 'The passing game was born here' reads a sign clamped to an adjacent iron fence. 'Hampden Bowling Club', it continues, 'sits on the site of the first Hampden Park'. Here, then, somewhere beneath the manicured lawn where Margaret and Joan and Jim and Willie aim for the jack, the Scotch Professors first passed and moved. No venue could be more apt for hosting the opening draw of the Scottish Cup in its 150th year. Here is an anniversary being marked in the presence of approving ghosts in baggy shorts.

It is a thrill to be there when the numbered balls clack. The sound is keener, crisper than on television – the difference between hearing a song live and listening through headphones. They grumble like a giant's starving belly when rifled through by those making the draw (today Colleen and Jack from the brilliant Street Soccer Scotland charity, both at first pulling out the numbers with the glee of children grabbing toys from breakfast cereal boxes). Then, as balls are plucked there follows a satisfying, comforting clatter akin to that of seaside pebbles clashing. Otherwise all is hushed, reverent, a church during prayers. It is even possible to hear those decisive marbles being placed in their craters.

The decisions those balls make scatter Bluebells and Swifts, Roses and Thistles, Shipyards and Welfares, Stars and Wanderers across Scotland. The ties conjured are for qualifying round matches. Beginning in the late summer teams from old pit villages and rural idylls will be lured by the Cup's everlasting charm. From hamlet to Hampden we will join them, along the way watching Bleachers and Belters, Loons and Mighty Mariners bloom then wither, giving way to the high and mighty of Edinburgh and Glasgow.

Come along with us now, we've a train to catch...

PRELIMINARY ROUNDS

CHAPTER 1

FEATURING

LUNCARTY V LOCH NESS
*12 August 2023,
Brownlands Park*

POLLOK V BENBURB
*2 September 2023
Newlandsfield Park*

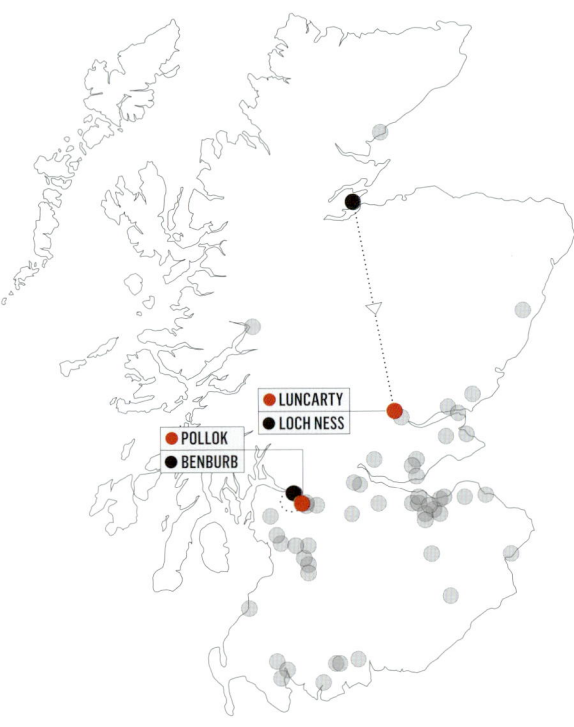

Preliminary Rounds One and Two involved a total of 55 clubs from East of Scotland League, West of Scotland League, Midlands League, North Caledonian League, North Region Junior Football League, South of Scotland League and Kingdom of Fife AFA

Two men and a dog at Brownlands Park, home of Luncarty FC.

CHAPTER 1

VILLAGE PEOPLE

And so it begins... Over two late summer weekends, 55 teams plucked from across the land joust to make the first round proper. Our journey starts beneath a village viaduct.

Luncarty and Loch Ness leaving the changing rooms at Luncarty's Brownlands Park.

A pair of Perthshire ladies shuffled uncomfortably as they awaited the number 34 to Stanley. They were perched upon the bus shelter's spartan metal beam bench, two budgies sharing a swing for one. The elder woman ran through a list of drinks she disliked. "Tea. Coffee. Ovaltine. Mulled wine. Anything hot, really." "But we go for Afternoon Tea every week!" replied her accomplice. "Yes, but I don't really enjoy it. It's just a habit, isn't it." A silence descended and was perhaps spent in mutual thoughts of regret at time wasted. I stood reflecting on how that last line sounded like a description of supporting a football team.

The bus spluttered into view and we were all soon seated and distracted by a pensioner who boarded before loudly announcing, "Jesus Christ, driver. It's stifling oan here. Are ye' trying to kill us all?" It was a strange way to say hello, but a greeting nonetheless. He sidled down the aisle, grabbing at and then opening a window on each side as he went, a rockpool crab nipping prying fingers.

Soon, hot air from the bus's floor-level ventilation system clashed with cool headwinds whooshing in through the windows and created a weather front over the heads of the scowling Afternoon Tea women. This tempestuous microclimate reflected meteorological conditions outside. One minute rain fell like marbles launched from a bully's slingshot; the next, radiant sunshine reigned. It should have been annoying, but few things seem to make us happier than saying "It just can't make its mind up, can it" to strangers on a bus.

As we nudged the Perth edgelands, I noticed a road sign for McDiarmid Park. On a cup tie day, it prompted thoughts of St Johnstone's recent prowess in this competition, and the

> *Half a dozen lone men cantered towards the ground. Each possessed the unmistakable demeanour of someone who simply had to be at football, no matter where.*

Left: Painting the lines in preparation for the Scottish Cup first preliminary round.

peculiar nature of their 2021 trophy win. That fine achievement had been hollowed by the absence of supporters with all their hollers, cheers and nonsense; 10,000 brides and grooms missing their own wedding days. When I pictured that empty Hampden final, I imagined players making crowd noises and saluting fictitious terraces, as if transported back to their childhood parks and gardens.

Up among the pebbledash bungalows of Luncarty, a few miles north of Perth, I left behind the Afternoon Tea duo – now silently looking out of opposing windows – and alighted by a field. On its sopping turf, teenage Scouts tried to care about a game involving ropes and ladders. Other locals studied a noticeboard outside the Spar shop and vacuumed up gossip. This was village football. From hamlet to Hampden, our Scottish Cup journey had begun.

Half a dozen lone men cantered towards the ground. Each possessed the unmistakable demeanour of someone who simply *had* to be at football, no matter where. They were members of the Saturday restless, a breed who need to be travelling in search of turnstiles to push, team sheets to gather and neatly fold, piping polystyrene cups to blow on, matches to enjoy with no inkling towards either team. Call them groundhoppers, call them what you like; they add numbers to attendance figures and income sheets, and are another detail in our game's intricate mural.

Right: The B-Boys of Luncarty FC await the whistle which will kick off the 150th Anniversary Season of the Scottish Cup.

Disaster for Loch Ness as Luncarty take the lead.

They had reason to choose Luncarty versus Loch Ness, reason beyond Brownlands Park's idyllic setting. This was the first time both clubs would compete in the Scottish Cup. History beneath the Highland Main Line. Victors in this first preliminary round would meet Newton Stewart. Hampden was two clock changes away, a remote universe in terms of footballing ability, and not for many rounds more would clubs advertise their child concessionary prices as 'Hee-haw' like Luncarty had; but still this was the cup, the same cup, the oldest cup in the world. "This is what it's all about, fairytales and dreams," home manager Jason McCrindle said before the game McCrindle had admitted to knowing little of the visiting side. In these nascent stages of the competition, video analysis and next opponent scouting reports were remote concepts. This was a blind date, football pared back to its simple rudiments of us versus them.

At Brownlands Park, the Loch Ness team coach had nestled in by a convoy of motorhomes and caravans and a pile of discarded uPVC doors. A cheerful queue mustered in-between the social club beer garden and a small play yard, forcing some people to hop over an absconded plastic seesaw on their way to the gate. "Home of the Bleachers" proclaimed a yellow banner – across three centuries, most in this village were employed in whitening the cloth woven in Scotland's linen mills. From a beer garden bench, a man in his twenties barked "Have you brought Nessie?" to two fans in Loch Ness scarves. The first rolled his eyes in the manner of

Too Shy. Luncarty pushing Loch Ness back in the early stages of the match.

a primary teacher who had heard one too many schoolboy lies. The second shot back with two simple words.

Understandably, their club employs the monster on its badge and in shirt designs. This branding has invited interest from across the globe, although some international fans have been disappointed to find that Loch Ness play 10 miles north of the water, in Fortrose. Perhaps worldwide shirt sales will one day raise enough funds for a floating pitch in the manner of the Albert Dock This Morning weather map of the 1990s. Until such a day, Loch Ness's main connection with football will remain the great floodlight theft of 1933. That year, following the first "sighting" of Nessie, pylons and bulbs used previously to illuminate fixtures at Caledonian FC's Telford Street ground were borrowed so that locals might look for the beast on dark winter nights. They were never returned.

Back by the Luncarty line, suited committee men – that sturdy stock who give us games to go to – said their hellos and expressed their wishes that the rain would hold off. One such jovial figure took gate money from a small shed. His shiplap billet doubled as the three-item club shop. A small boy arrived, waggled a £10 note and asked to buy a scarf. There was only one in stock. "This one's got a bit of dust on it," said the man, giving it a shake. "Tell ye' what. Just give us a fiver for it." Happily confused, the boy walked away, scarf in one hand and spare fiver in the other. He paused momentarily in front of another shed whose offerings included £1.50 bags of assorted sweets, then walked on. For

The red wall. Loch Ness fans watching on at Brownlands Park.

those 20 seconds, it was almost possible to see a cartoon-style thought bubble above his head.

On three sides of bucolic Brownlands, grass banking gave the feeling of being in a minor amphitheatre – perhaps a venue in the Roman non-league. Thoughts of empire were thickened by the viaduct that looms magnificently over this entire site.

Eighty or so people gathered on the highest bank, in front of the sheds and dressing rooms and looking down onto a goal end. Among them were grandads in charge of prams, nanas chasing toddlers and teenagers trying not to be caught showing enthusiasm for anything. This mix of people and the cheery hubbub they produced made for a village fete atmosphere. Then the teams marched out and a man in his fifties bellowed, "Fucking intae these, Luncarty." As the referee counted to 22, clouds segregated, uncloaking a sky of gladdening blue. Suddenly, the sun raged, fat and splendid.

During the first few minutes of the game, steam submerged the viaduct. These were not the offerings of an old locomotive – though a 125 did trundle by, its driver, you hope, checking in on the match – but smoke signals from the Luncarty Ultras. In a far-flung corner away from the fete, this band of 20 or so local teens lit their flares and thumped their drums. Their existence could be taken as a surprise or a curiosity at this level of the game, but it is neither. All across lower league football can be found tribes like this, perhaps priced out by loftier venues and finding unity and belonging for "hee-haw" or a few quid in happy places like this.

Wearing waspish colours Luncarty dominated their northern visitors in rioja red. It was perhaps this swarm – or the behind goal advertisement for Andy Law Pest Control, "Wasp elimination guaranteed" – that led one woman near me to offer an update on her household insect problems. "The wasps are back, Annie," she said. "I told you they would be." Annie nodded and then complained about how boring football is when the action is at the other end. "They should just have two balls on the pitch," she added, "That'd liven it up."

The home side's assault continued. A free-kick careered across goal like a saucepan lid hurled by an angry chef. Winger Kyle Woolley glided through on goal but muddled his one-on-one chance. Bleach-haired Bleacher Rhys Davies hit a post. When the ball was cast forward, Loch Ness's Phil MacDonald – a handsome hirsute type with the prickly aura of a Viking on shore leave – chased fervently but fruitlessly. His team became frustrated. A free-kick was awarded to Luncarty and Ness midfielder Allan McPhee punched the ball into the ground as if playing volleyball with the devil. A refused penalty plea worsened matters. The Viking looked mad enough to pillage Tizer and Space Raiders from the catering shed.

That spot-kick should probably have been given, as should one for the home side moments later. On both occasions, the referee shook his head vigorously from side to side as if watching a table tennis match no-one else could see. The Luncarty Ultras screamed in anger. The troop probably would have let off another flare, but it became obvious that they had none left. They quietened somewhat, perhaps into that malaise of rueful reflection many of us enter having eaten our packed lunch too early on a long train journey. For a while the game joined them in the doldrums. Midfielders pinged passes to ghosts in yards of space, defenders donked clearances out of play. The latter, at least, created an entertaining sport of its own as amateur ball

> **During the first few minutes of the game, steam submerged the viaduct. These were not the offerings of an old locomotive checking in on the match … but smoke signals from the Luncarty Ultras.**

Chapter 1 | Cup Tied | 21

boys and girls competed to retrieve the Size 5 from the foliage, small gangs hunting down prey.

Then, finally, goals to cheer. Two of them: a jabbed finish by Woolley followed by some Davies incision. The latter player was a cut above all afternoon, strutting when others waded. At half-time a man behind me in the tea bar queue referred to him as "the Luncarty Haaland". Nearby, children roly-polyed down the steepest grass bank and a club volunteer with a "Jesus Saves" style stick and board paraded today's winning prize draw numbers. It is not often that football makes you sigh contentedly, but Brownlands Park during the early flames of the Scottish Cup did just that.

The sun smashed through unremittingly in the second half, heightening this agreeable mood. Then quite rudely Josh Race – grandson of Roy, we may hope – scored for Loch Ness. A hitherto tranquil posse of away fans roared gutturally. This tie was not yet dead. And then it was. Jamie Mackie scored Luncarty's third.

Soon the last whistle peeped and cheers echoed from the viaduct arches. Moments later behind the goal, the referee wished Loch Ness supporters a safe journey home. Football can be a pleasant little outing.

A few weeks later, and with summer not yet giving up its lease to autumn, Luncarty won through in the second preliminary round. A 4-1 victory down in Newton Stewart made The Bleachers' young cup run the talk of the village. Elsewhere, Wanderers and Thistles, Bluebells and Stars and Swifts collided. Goals troubled nets from Creetown to Culter. Auchinleck Talbot gathered a dozen in Wigtown, Clydebank 10 in Fort William. In Glasgow, Pollok and Benburb – local sides of fine and gritty vintage – could be separated only by a penalty shootout. On a warm and lucid September Saturday, the new, ancient Scottish Cup bristled with possibility. ●

RESULTS:
LUNCARTY 3, LOCH NESS 1
POLLOCK 2, BENBURB 2
POLLOCK WON ON PENALTIES 3-0

> **Soon the last whistle peeped and cheers echoed from the viaduct arches. Moments later behind the goal, the referee wished Loch Ness supporters a safe journey home. Football can be a pleasant little outing.**

More pressure from Luncarty during their 3-1 Scottish Cup win over Loch Ness.

A Loch Ness supporter wearing the club's iconic Nessie strip.

Jamie Mackie adds Luncarty's third to ensure their passage in to the next round of the cup.

Pollok take on Benburb in the 2nd Preliminary Round. Pollok win the tie 3-0 on penalties after a 2-2 draw.

Some rare late summer sun makes for tricky viewing.

Choose your end for the best view in the ground.

Benburb's second as they race to a 2-0 lead against the home team.

Half-time at Pollok's Newlandsfield Park. Time to change ends.

Chapter 1 | **Cup Tied** | 29

Benburb are inches away from taking a 3-0 lead against Pollok.

Made in the shade. Watching on as Pollok come back from two down to win 3-0 on penalties after extra time.

The best stand in Scottish Football. Looking over the garden fence with beer and fags.

FIRST ROUND

FEATURING

CAMELON JUNIORS v CIVIL SERVICE STROLLERS
23 September 2023
Carmuirs Park

UNIVERSITY OF STIRLING v ALBION ROVERS
25 September 2023,
Forthbank Stadium

CHAPTER 2

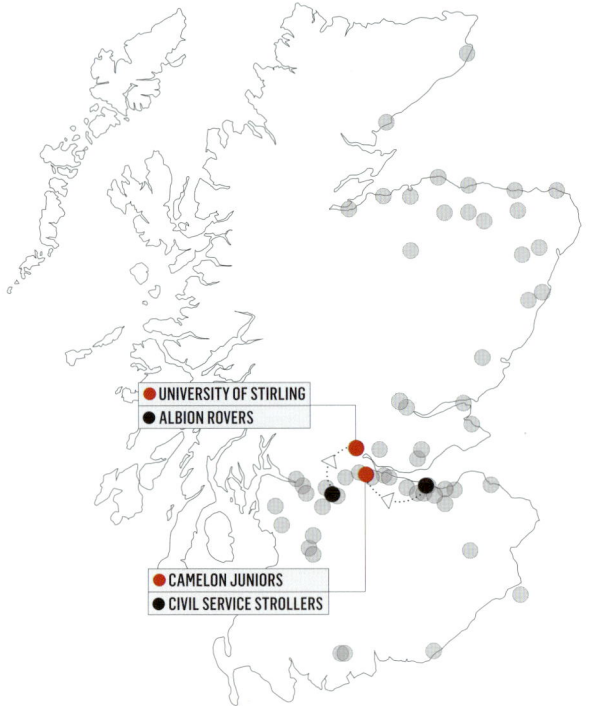

The First Round involved a total of 60 clubs from Highland League, Lowland League, East of Scotland League, West of Scotland League, Midlands League, North Caledonian League, North Region Junior Football League and South of Scotland League

32 | Cup Tied

CHAPTER 2

DREAMING BY THE OLD CANAL

Autumn drifts in and makes our game look golden as Highland and Lowland League clubs join the shindig. For our next stop, we moor up near Falkirk.

Two crows were perched on the lock gate, apparently deep in conversation. Perhaps they were remarking how this had once been a bustling junction at which the Forth & Clyde Canal from Glasgow met the Union from Edinburgh. There was a certain romance about the place too; by night, honeymooning couples would drift along on small barges known as "hoolets". Today, an abandoned vessel of Tupperware listed in the breezy, rippling water and a lad of 11 or 12 hurled pebbles at a floating Irn Bru can in an attempt to sink it. It was an appropriate berth for the drink tin – not 10 metres away loitered a silhouette statue of Robert Barr, local soft drink magnate and Father of the Bru.

Red Admiral butterflies scuttled through the air. Soon, they would be scarpering for milder climes and not returning until this competition had entered its Hampden phase. Foliage had turned rusty, flowers wilted and the sun dropped a notch in height and radiance. Here was autumn; proper football time.

We were on the towpath, dawdling among fixated joggers and idling dog walkers, because it skirted Carmuirs Park, home of Camelon Juniors FC. From here, it was possible to glance through wispy fern trees and into The Mariners' cheerful red-roofed home. There, players thudded pre-match warm up passes to one another and walloped shots onto the hospitality hut roof. The Tannoy croaked into life, blasting Rag 'n' Bone man's 'Giant' across the canal with an unlikely ferocity that caused a cyclist to wobble and almost plunge into the water.

Positioned next to the Forth and Clyde Canal, Camelon's Carmuirs Park is ready to host the first round tie against Civil Service Strollers.

Around the corner among the pebbledash homes of Carmuirs Avenue, a lone red and white Mariners flag flopped from a bedroom window. There was a sense not so much of cup fever, but a mild case of the sniffles. Outside the Camelon Juniors social club, a man looked over and raised his cigarette in welcoming salute, as if it were a top hat or an ornamental cane.

Beyond the blood red iron turnstiles an old

Pre-match snacks at Angie's Cafe.

man sold lotto tickets from a trestle table, that staple furniture piece of non-league football. He greeted by name each home fan who arrived, an amiable concierge in a flat cap and sensible cagoule rather than a tailcoat and fancy hat. Those who spoke with him could not help but look over his shoulder in the manner of somebody spotting that a celebrity has walked into a room. For there behind the lotto man was the radiant turf, lush at this time of year just as a September country field is bountiful before harvest. A club record – 'The Mariners Song', a sort of canal shanty – played, the sun mustered some spirit and once more the Scottish Cup felt like a village fete or a church garden party.

From the concrete terrace running alongside the pitch, it was possible to see into the gardens of neighbouring houses. There was activity in one, as a man wearing a Camelon shirt entered what seemed at first to be a shed and then raised a viewing flap. Soon, he was joined in his handcrafted shiplap grandstand by a friend. As the referee tooted the game into life, both opened cans of lager and gave cheers to their simple genius.

Behind the other goal and yet to reach an age when sheds excite, more boisterous ultras had gathered. Aged from the last years of primary school to the early stages of secondary, this ragtag squadron sang for town and team, thrashed a drum and waved flags with the unremitting enthusiasm of North Korean soldiers on military parade day. Their megaphone bearer had a weakness for using his

instrument's siren facility to perturb the visiting keeper, so that goal kicks now summoned to mind air raid warnings. Their repertoire included a hearty chorus of "Camelon 'til I die" and an impromptu round of "Who's the ginger on the floor?" after a Strollers player had, in their view, taken an exaggerated fall in the box. They sang too a tune based on Manfred Mann's 'Do Wah Diddy Diddy', led on the megaphone by one teenage boy with a particularly strong Falkirk accent. In such moments, watching the Camelon Ultras was a bit like stumbling upon on an avant-garde band in the basement of a Berlin

The long march. Changing ends at half-time.

bar, or watching certain iterations of The Fall.

By contrast, the Strollers were backed by a lone fan. Raiding solo from Edinburgh, he was a middle-aged man with a carrier bag – another ubiquitous mainstay of lower level football. Rather than shrink into the background as might be expected, for much of the game he vigorously howled for his team, a solitary foghorn who thrashed at an advertising hoarding as if manning barricades during the French Revolution. When his side rattled a post early on, his epic, guttural cry of "Oooooooh!" threatened to rekindle some ancient tribal feud in a faraway rainforest. His enthusiasm was not admired by everyone. Several times, small groups of home supporters stood near him but soon moved on as the volcano erupted. They departed furtively and self-consciously, like the members of a family changing their minds and leaving a restaurant before ordering.

The admirable Stollers One, the shed men and the teenage wailers were treated to a frenetic

Delight for the Camelon Ultras as their team is awarded a penalty.

Camelon and Civil Service Strollers in the first round at Carmuirs Park.

> **Behind the goal at half-time, a Dalmatian pottered and a dad played What Time Is It Mr Wolf? with his daughter.**

first 15 minutes in which both teams' forward players darted around hysterically as if being chased by spindles of fork lightning. Soon the game slowed and I took to pondering the away team's name and heritage. Were any of the modern squad acting civil servants? It was possible to imagine a number of them in certain roles. Their striker, CSS10, had the air of a young mailroom porter susceptible to practical jokes from senior colleagues. Captain CSS4 resembled a senior I.T. officer much admired for his policy of bringing in breakfast rolls on a Friday.

What did not fit my civil service hypothesising was the Strollers' heretical, anarchic approach to shirt numbering: employing number two as a left-back and three at right-back surely contravened numerous protocols and policies. Then the calamitous clunk of a match ball landing upon a corrugated roof shook me awake, a vintage and treasured sound of early cup rounds. As it rolled back to earth, the ball made the noise of a beer keg travelling from street to cellar.

When play returned, that browbeaten ball was clipped long towards the Mariners' penalty area. The wiry CSS10 scampered underneath it but was bumped dodgem-like by Ryan McElwee, a home defender. The Strollers forward sprawled on the turf, arms and legs outstretched in the manner of a Looney Toons character falling from a cliff. Penalty. Even the squawking megaphone siren could not perturb CSS8 from scoring.

The Strollers now dominated. CSS10 threatened and bothered the Camelon backline, a nagging presence. Often left lonely by teammates, he whittled chances for himself, including one shot that was spooned spectacularly over the bar. "How shit must you

> **In the second half I moved to the shed end. Its owner had built this, surely football's tiniest enclosure, five years ago. For the price of returning errant footballs, he and his neighbour were allowed to watch without charge.**

be?" sang the ultras, "It's hit someone's car."

Behind the goal at half-time, a Dalmatian pottered and a dad played What Time Is It Mr Wolf? with his daughter. Teenagers queued for Steak and Buckfast pies while winning lotto numbers and prizes snared were announced to a soundtrack of 'Children' by Robert Miles, a somewhat earthy yet psychedelic remix.

In the second half I moved to the shed end. Its owner had built this, surely football's tiniest enclosure, five years ago. For the price of returning errant footballs, he and his neighbour were allowed to watch without charge. They saw nothing eccentric or novel in their pursuit, and hadn't even noticed the stickers slapped beneath their viewing hatch by visitors from Copenhagen and Hamburg. Instead, they saw only the game and the Scottish Cup's unending possibilities. "We're still in this," said one shed man, "Plenty of time." For football fans watching from terraces, plastic seats or garden benches, there is always still time.

Early in the second half, from their observation hide they watched as another penalty was awarded, this time for Camelon. As Sam Collumbine placed the ball on the spot, a hush shrouded the ground. It seemed more fitting of the stasis before a match-winning serve at Wimbledon. All that could be heard was a rare barge chugging along the canal. Collumbine scored and for a few seconds this parcel of land on the edge of Falkirk seemed like one of the happiest places on earth.

The Mariners swelled forwards to find another goal, squashing their opponents. The Strollers seemed trapped, spiders captured in a glass. Yet all the home side's diligence amounted to nothing. Suddenly, and rude as an unwanted guest, the Strollers were awarded another penalty, in front of the shed. As one, the ultras battalion sprinted through the main stand and arrived in time to try and irritate Strollers' CSS10 into a miss. Their mission failed. Beneath the pine trees the visiting side had their winner.

"That was never a penalty, the referee just wants to get home for his tea," said an old man as we trudged from the ground. Such a low level, gentle conspiracy theory befitted this pleasant creed of football down by the canal.

Round one of the cup sprawled into Monday, when we watched academics falter in the presence of vintage Rovers, finalists just over a century ago. There were no ultras among the breezeblock stands of Stirling, but instead gaggles of students filing in late and wondering how best to make chants of the word 'university'. Yet this difference was a filament of this competition's gift: from shed men to plastic carrier soloists, as autumn encroached and butterflies departed, it remained a tapestry of a competition. ●

RESULTS:
CAMELON JUNIORS 1, CIVIL SERVICE STROLLERS 2
UNIVERSITY OF STIRLING 1, ALBION ROVERS 3

It's five to three and the last supporters enter Carmuirs Park.

Watching from the corners as Civil Service Strollers defeat Camelon 2-1 in a match of three penalty kick goals.

Roll out the red paint. Last minute touch-ups for Carmuirs Park for the Scottish Cup first round.

Handing out flags and banners to the University of Stirling fans.

Goalmouth scramble under a supermoon as Stirling University take on Albion Rovers in the first round of the cup.

BBC Scotland kick off their 23/24 Scottish Cup coverage at Forthbank for the first round match between Stirling University and Albion Rovers.

The TV cameras are in attendance for the Stirling University v Albion Rovers first round match.

It would have been an autograph once, but now the football player selfie rules.

The young team cheering on Albion Rovers with a second round place at stake.

All smiles for these Albion Rovers fans as they beat Stirling University 3-1 to progress to the second round.

SECOND ROUND

FEATURING

TRANENT V EAST KILBRIDE
28 October 2023
Foresters Park

MUSSELBURGH ATHLETIC V CLYDE
30 October 2023
Olivebank

3
CHAPTER

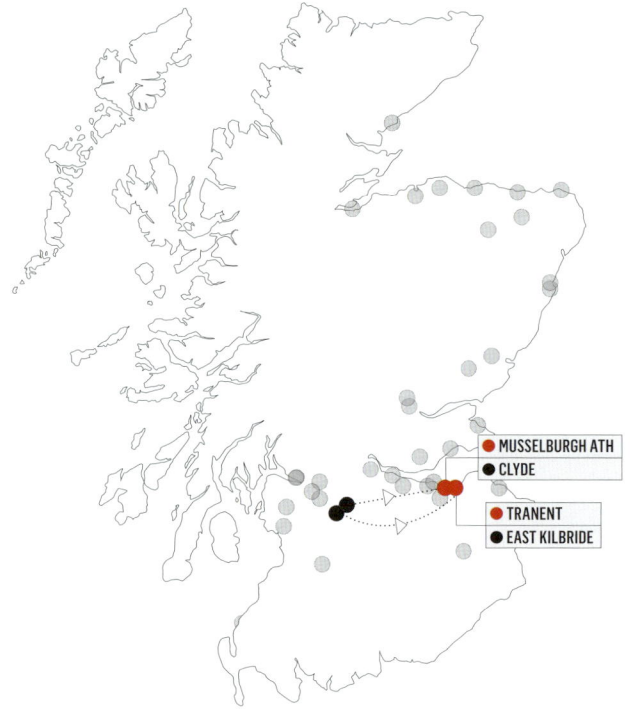

The Second Round involved a total of 40 clubs from League Two, Highland League, Lowland League, East of Scotland League and West of Scotland League

The only fireworks for the first hour were the premature ones for Guy Fawkes Night.

CHAPTER 3

MUSSEL MUSEUM

With the changing of the clocks arrive chilly evenings perfect for floodlit dreaming. In the Lothians we find unexpected goals aplenty...

The man wore a bobble hat, though its bobble was missing. "There I was, walking to the game and it just flew off, into the sea," he explained in a Lancastrian accent. This uninvited fashion alteration had created a beanie hat with three orange wool tufts where the bobble once was. "It was only a few quid but it'd done 97 grounds."

The Scottish Cup is magnetic to groundhoppers, an irresistible and compelling force. Although they could visit and tick off this nation's smaller football venues at any time, there is an allure to watching cup games staged within them. That appeal is thickened when a non-league side are hosting a professional club, as would be the case this evening in Musselburgh, whose hungry waters had consumed the bobble. Further, despite the passing of much time since their finest years either side of the Second World War, the home side's opponents, Clyde, retained a dishevelled form of glamour having thrice won the Scottish Cup. It awarded watching the League Two club in this competition a voyeuristic intrigue, like looking at tabloid photographs of celebrities who had fallen on hard times.

Some of the groundhoppers had constructed an entire long weekend around the Cup, its second round draw determining that part of a minibreak be spent in Kilwinning or Huntly. They had been there too as we had watched the Belters of Tranent lash East Kilbride 7-0, a result that in its scale represented a different shape of cup shock to the usual. Now, visitors and residents of the Honest Toun would be among the 1,000 people filling Musselburgh's gently named Olivebank ground. The game was a sell-out of the type that would once have been referred to as "a good night for local burglars", except the local burglars had tickets too.

All of us walked beneath this black night's aloof moonlight towards inviting, glossy pylons.

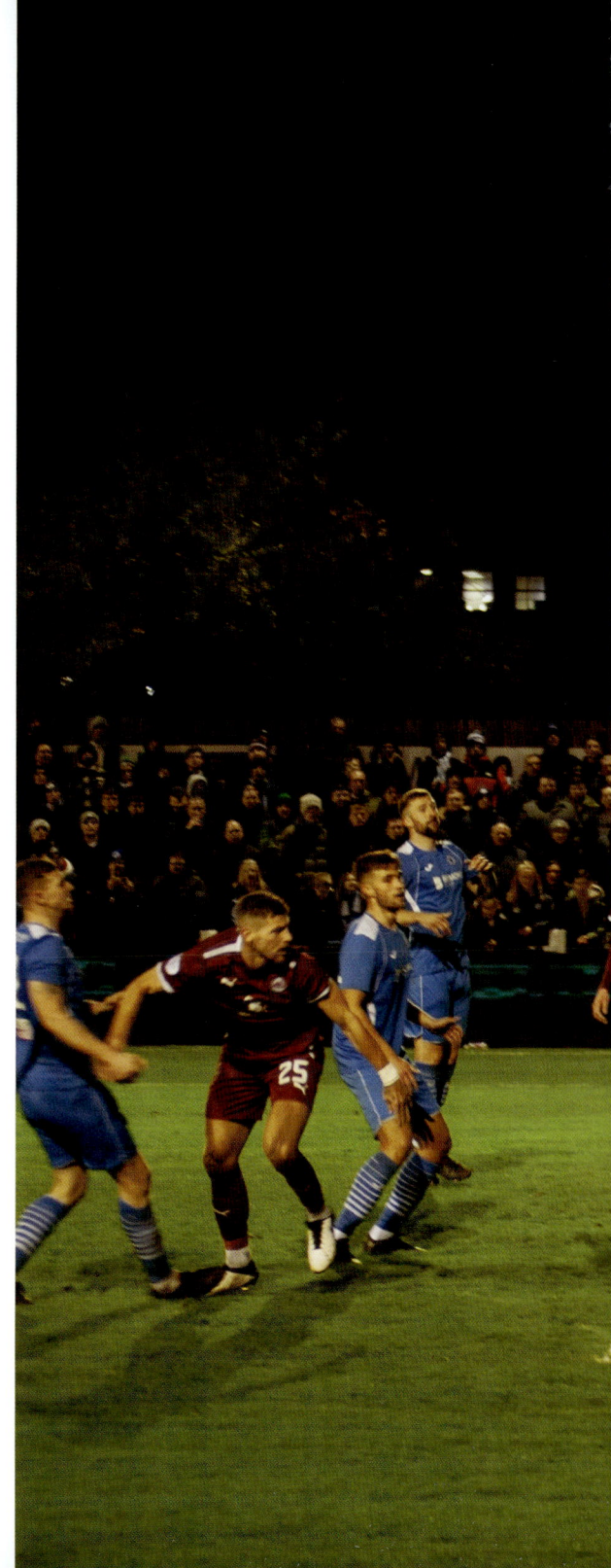

Goalmouth scramble at Olivebank as Musselburgh take on Clyde in this Scottish Cup second round clash.

Mimicking the Subbuteo TV Tower from the 1980s the BBC Scotland cameras look on as Clyde defeat Musselburgh 3-2.

> **All of us walked beneath this black night's aloof moonlight towards inviting, glossy pylons. Floodlights were a guide, delivering us through a mysterious narrow passage to the broad certainty of the ground.**

Floodlights were a guide, delivering us through a mysterious narrow passage to the broad certainty of the ground. An old lady watched the passing flock from behind her garden wall. It was impossible to imagine her doing so for humdrum league games. She craned her neck to watch the street theatre: old soldiers in berets holding buckets and pinning Remembrance Poppies with shaky fingers; programme sellers exclaiming their wares like one-story town criers; volunteers offering lotto tickets and "guess the team" football cards with the gusto of Victorian fairground ride proprietors; club officials in manicured suits checking lists and giving thumbs-ups to civvy street acquaintances. At this time tomorrow, there would be nothing here but seagulls jabbing with their beaks at discarded ketchup sachets.

On the other side of the gates, locals arrived and marvelled at the crowd: "Half the toun's in!" and "Jeez, ah've never seen it like this." They saluted neighbours and people from work and parents recognised from the school run, mouthing and gesticulating admiration at this bustling scene. No one could tell Musselburgh people that the Scottish Cup did not matter so much anymore.

Some shuffled over to the steep grass bank which accompanies one side of the pitch and took shelter under trees from rain now growing in confidence. Others squashed themselves onto the museum piece terrace opposite, shielded by its cowshed roof. It was a vintage backdrop that was suddenly undermined when electronic pitchside advertising hoardings flickered into life. They were incongruous, like spotting a Sky TV dish on a nunnery roof.

After the coin toss, the two teams changed ends, a lesser-spotted phenomenon in modern football. Usually, this manoeuvre – commanded by the visiting captain – is enough to cause panic in the stands. Superstition dictates that by shooting "the wrong way" the natural order is distorted and our team is almost certain to lose. Yet at Olivebank there were no such qualms. Instead, home supporters throatily spurred on their men as they flitted across the pitch. The noise they made carried the unquestioning backing of parents on school sports day. In response, 100 or so followers of Clyde announced in song that "We're the Bully Wee."

Up front for Musselburgh, Kris Renton made a physical declaration of his presence by ruffling opponent centre-half Peter Grant as if attempting to sculpt him like plasticine. Then the home captain, Declan O'Kane, thundered into a challenge on Bully Wee forward Martin Rennie. The collision of his boot with the ball made the sound of an iceberg breaking. "That'll put hairs on his chest" said a man near me in reference to Rennie, an interesting concept to ponder. Musselburgh, though, were not merely purveyors of industrial brawn. Right wing-back Craig Stevenson struck a decadent shot with the outside of his boot which almost sailed home. O'Kane spun around the breed of long passes which call to mind an expert angler casting masterfully.

And then... nothing. For at least 20 minutes until half time the game descended into a formless blancmange. The ball seldom seemed to leave the middle third of the pitch or rest with one team's players for long. It was as if both sides were embarrassed by it. "Find feet," repeated the man next to me over and over again, a despairing mantra. Instead, Clyde's Erik Šuľa passed the ball out of play having apparently spotted a teammate lingering in the snaking catering hatch queue. Soon afterwards came the sweet release of the referee's whistle. "Is it always this bad?" asked a middle-aged woman in that queue. "Aye," replied her partner, "But there's usually nae queue for a pie."

Clyde began the second half brimming with fine intentions. They passed briskly and moved around the pitch with verve, children in the playground after a morning of maths. It was as if they were trying to play football from a higher level or another time. Yet they were foiled, often by resolute Musselburgh defending, and often by dense, quicksand turf which frequently tripped up their play. Disheartened, they seemed almost

Glengarry and Beret-clad men clutch coffee or Bovril to keep out the chill of a dark night in Musselburgh.

innocent bystanders as the match degenerated into a state of boggy disharmony. From somewhere outside the ground, a firework exploded and lit the sky behind one goal spectacularly. It seemed like an act of sarcasm.

What happened next – over the final 15 minutes of the 90 and the half hour of extra time which followed – was, in this context, extraordinary. That these clumsy teams could muster five goals must amount to a miracle. Here was a desert mirage which turned out to be real.

First, Clyde took the lead after three alarmingly exquisite snappy passes on the penalty area's edge that gave Connor Young the prompt to ping home. Now rain lashed down and the Honest Toun's dream faded. O'Kane, however, had faith and ability enough to hoist a wholesome free-kick into the box. There, defender Jamie Todd climbed telescopically and with his forehead pummelled the ball into the net. One-all, local elation and extra time.

Across Olivebank, parents decided that yawns in class tomorrow would be worth it: their children needed to see the moment when little old Burgh humbled a league team. Yet for all the fairy tales that football authors, it snuffs many more others. Rennie made it 2-1 to Clyde, Kian Leslie added another. Renton replied for the home team but the goal arrived so belatedly that even the customary grabbing of the ball from the net by his teammates seemed an act of ritual rather than hope.

Soon they were trudging from the pitch. Each man looked as if he had lost the bobble from his favourite hat. ●

RESULTS:
MUSSELBURGH ATHLETIC 2, CLYDE 3
TRANENT 7, EAST KILBRIDE 0

Not much goalmouth, but plenty of byline action before the match exploded into a 3-2 thriller in Clyde's favour.

56 | Cup Tied | Chapter 3

Every ground should have one – the 'Next Home Game' sign at Tranent FC's Foresters Park.

Fans entering Foresters Park for the second round Scottish Cup match between Tranent and East Kilbride.

"Who Are We?" – You are very definitely Tranent FC.

As good a way to see that team sheet as you are going to get.

Chapter 3 | Cup Tied | 61

Fans in the Main Stand at Tranent's Foresters Park look on as their team triumph 7-0.

The octagonal 1960's St Martins of Tours church is the backdrop to this goalmouth stramash.

'And a-one, and a-two, and a-one two three four'. The Tranent Big T-Bois keeping it real.

Kallum Higginbotham wheels away after scoring the final goal in Tranent's 7-0 demolishing of East Kilbride.

The team of tomorrow look on.

Tin-foil flags for the Big T-Bois.

The Big T Snack Bar at Tranent FC's Foresters Park.

THIRD ROUND

FEATURING

DUNFERMLINE V RAITH ROVERS
24 November 2023
East End Park

PETERHEAD V AYR UNITED
25 November 2023
Balmoor Stadium

The Third Round involved a total of 40 clubs from the Championship, League One, League Two, Highland League, Lowland League, East of Scotland League and West of Scotland League

Sammy the Tammy, Dunfermline's large-headed mascot, gets the atmosphere going before the third round game against Raith Rovers.

CHAPTER 4

TOONLIGHT SERENADE

Teams from the Championship and League One clock on, though 13 non-league sides remain. To the bright side of Fife we go for a floodlit Friday, and then north to see some fishermen's blues.

On a sharp winter's evening, they paraded down the Halbeath Road summoned by floodlights. At a certain point, the glow of East End Park transformed them into silhouettes, as if they had crossed into another realm. In a sense, they had: going to the match springs us from this world into an altogether different other. Not that this other place sparkles with lofty enlightenment and optimism. "It gets earlier every bloody year," said one Dunfermline supporter to his friend. "Christmas?", came the reply. "Nah. Us getting knocked out of the cup."

Inside, we all looked to turf rendered luminous by pylon and bulb. It blazed like some giant Post-It Note with line markings instead of scribblings. On nights like these, football pitches are our sunshine in winter. Pars followers once again flung grit among the celestial, this time with a specially adapted version of 'Always Look on the Bright Side of Life': "Rovers live on the shite side of Fife," they chorused. Visitors from Kirkcaldy responded by eagerly booing the Pars furry mascot, Sammy the Tammy. This, after all, was a derby. A derby under the lights. A *Cup* derby under the lights. High days and holidays have been declared for less.

Season-ticket holders said their fortnightly hellos and shook hands heartily just as the players of Dunfermline and Raith did so frostily on the pitch. Each battalion of ultras held, then hurled, their flares. Smoke engulfed players, who now resembled moorland hikers stranded by a sudden fog. The air smelt of spent cap gun cartridges and the morning after Bonfire Night.

The Pars were groggy, Rovers sprightly. In Aidan Connolly and Dylan Easton, they possessed a couple of slight and wispy forwards who were only two sets of baggy shorts away from throwing

Light and Lines. The geometry of football stadiums.

The old-school charm of Dunfermline's East End Park prior to the third round clash with Raith Rovers.

us back to the 1920s, and players who knew this cup in its fifties. For Dunfermline, Owen Moffat – low socks, palms outstretched beseeching teammates for the ball – stirred home noise with his endeavours. Then Easton whirled through the defence, apparently passing to himself in the manner of a player in a grandad's far-fetched story, and crossed for Jack Hamilton to score. Invaders from the Lang Toun found themselves suddenly berserk. Seats were clambered and shin-bones rapped. An orange flare made it to the pitch and flickered lazily like a lost roadworks lamp.

Rovers now cruised largely through the direction of midfielder Sam Stanton, something of an engineer identifying problems, curtailing them and devising something better. His sudden blasts forward were like those of a sheepdog under command. Otherwise, the game entered a period of fallow nothingness. Full-backs swished and smashed forwards balls that no striker this side of Brazil 1970 could hope to bring under command. Dunfermline huffed and puffed beneath cries from the stand of "Hit it!" whenever they reached within bothering distance of the goal. Nearby, a man released the exaggerated yawn of someone trying to rid his lounge of guests, perhaps practising for Christmas. Thankfully, referee Willie Collum blew the half-time whistle and the players obliged the yawn by departing.

Early in the second half, Dunfermline rustled into life. They were propelled by Moffat, a spinning top zigzagging between opponents. Rovers, though, sat calm and awaited their turn to advance. Soon, Josh Mullin cast a set-piece into the box and Stanton clouted home. Then, directly from another free-kick Lewis Vaughan scored for 0-3. Coiled in from close to the corner of the penalty area, it was an artwork that inspired hysteria in the away end.

Unable to ingest further heartbreak and goading, many home supporters left. As if agreeing with their decision, Dunfermline missed a late penalty. Fife had turned blue and Raith – cantering in the league – now found themselves partial to a cup run. For us, though, it was time to hit the north.

Triangles and 3v3 as Dunfermline try to force an opening against Raith.

> **Full-backs swished and smashed forwards balls that no striker this side of Brazil 1970 could hope to bring under command. Dunfermline huffed and puffed beneath cries from the stand of "Hit it!" whenever they reached within bothering distance of the goal.**

Delight for these Raith fans as Dunfermline miss a late penalty.

3-0 up away from home in the cup, against your local rivals.

> **In the Blue Toon, the sky had turned the colour of a wizened gravestone and the North Sea now resembled a vast field of paving stone rubble.**

The next morning, from Aberdeen we took a bus north beneath magnificent skies of split personality, in one corner glum and in another hopeful. Road signs offered up Ducuick and Tippety, Oldmeldrum and Tarsets, Berryslacks and Hardslacks; location names that had fallen out of a Victorian novel and onto the map. On the outskirts of Ellon, cold-handed golfers dreamt of Saturday night takeaways and spring. The clock had not yet struck one but they were playing in the unreliable and pale glow of an energy efficient lightbulb shortly before it expires.

This was surely football's time of year, and not that of five irons and dubious trousers. The cup draw had sent urban Pollok people more than 200 miles north to the pastures of Brora; Formartine were fleeing south for Falkirk; and Ayr setting out on a cross country orienteering trek to Peterhead. All of them were seeds scattered in the wind. We let the breeze take us along to Balmoor with those marauding Honest Men; League Two against the Championship, hopes of a cup shock against dull rationalism.

In the Blue Toon, the sky had turned the colour of a wizened gravestone and the North Sea now resembled a vast field of paving stone rubble. I longed for the dark of last night and four floodlights' promising glow. Sometimes winter is better left unseen. From the shuttered doorway of Vivas nightclub, a man in a blue Peterhead beanie hat warned seagulls against encroaching on his bag of chips. He shooed a particularly adamant trespasser deftly with his right foot, as if nudging a quick free-kick sideways to an onrushing teammate. "Away!" he pleaded, "Gies peace."

Lengthy Queen Street was studded with further home supporters in blue headwear. Their bobbing nappers were bright sirens in the murk and cheerful buoys leading us home to Balmoor. There, arrivals encountered the usual football ground society of programme sellers and ratcheting turnstiles, of passing conversations predicting narrow wins and kids pulling parental hands towards kick-off. To leave a vacant town centre and be landed suddenly here was like happening upon a big top circus in some polar outpost. Football gives life.

Beyond the gates, standing on Balmoor's merry courtyard with its pie shed and club shop hut, I feared for the chips man from Vivas. Bounding among us all was Peterhead's mascot – and namesake of his Dunfermline cousin – Sammy the Scurry, a gigantic seagull with Demon Headmaster eyes and the wingspan of a Lancaster bomber. Any encounter would surely

A fiery sunset over the clash between Peterhead and Ayr which sees the visitors run out 2-1 winners.

Many local trawlermen support Peterhead – Jock and the 'Lapwing' in this case.

Hot food on a cold Peterhead November afternoon.

send chips man into some kind of hideous conniption fit. Sammy was not of a size that could be manipulated with a shoe.

Old boys with faces furrowed and chiselled by the sea queued for their pre-match fuel; "R. Coutts & Son Butchers", boasted a painted sign, "Mid Street, Peterhead. Suppliers of Pies to Peterhead FC". Yet it could not be escaped that this was a club of the ocean and not the farm.

That much is there in the name – Saint Peter, patron saint of netmakers, shipbuilders and fishermen. Then there is the club crest, in which a haddock is pictured apparently nodding a ball into a goal. And on the wall behind an actual goal, large photographs of trawlers are accompanied by messages of support – Atlantic Challenge ("Owners & Crew wish their home team all the best."), Consortium ("Norman McLean and his crew are proud to support PFC") and more. Beyond Balmoor from that vantage can be seen only the colossal lone chimney of Peterhead Power Station, and then nothing but the North Sea. No fisherman truly escapes work here, even on the most mesmerising of Saturdays.

Our teams walked on and in the away end a scarlet flare was held aloft. Though gleaming and dramatic, it did not please two locals near me, who perhaps saw pyrotechnics as objects to be taken seriously in times of offshore peril. "They should just abandon a game when that happens," said one man and "It looks good but its no right," the other.

Pie and Bovril. The dream.

A long trip to Peterhead for these Ayr United fans.

> **30 or 40 kids from primary age to young teen, arms linked and bouncing, lost in the moment. "Blue Toooon/ Blue Toooon" was the cry.**

Both the Ayr ultras brandishing the flare and their Peterhead equivalents infused this compact ground with racket and fervour. The home contingent were a younger bunch – 30 or 40 kids from primary age to young teen, arms linked and bouncing, lost in the moment. "Blue Toooon/Blue Toooon" was the cry. If life in a fishing town is uncertain and occasionally frightening, then in a football club they had something steady and permanent. Plus, Balmoor gave them somewhere to shout "Wanker" at adults without fear of repercussions.

Ayr started efficiently, popping the ball between one another with the swiftness of a secret note being passed around a classroom. The home side darted after it, roused by their co-bosses Ryan Strachan and Jordon Brown.

The pair applauded heartily when Peterhead shoehorned in the first shot of the day, a curling number from one of few club stalwarts left in the game, Rory McAllister. Then Hamish Ritchie dribbled, slalomed and cajoled his way through the Ayr backline, before jabbing a shot wide. Some from the Blue Toon began to dream. They were quickly jolted back to reality by piercing sideways raindrops that seemed to attack in shoals. Soon, and for a good while, the game descended into a huff and puff quagmire of ducks chasing bread.

Sturdy Aiden McGeady, surely time travelling, strived to offer something more palatable. The former Celtic man smooched the ball with his feet, rolling it around as if doing an impression

Chapter 4 | Cup Tied | 81

> **In the main stand, an old man gestured towards Peterhead's pogoing young 'uns and remarked, "They're gonna end up with grumpy knees, that lot."**

of his flamboyant younger self. It was enjoyable to watch though often fizzled to nothing, a portion of shilly-shallying to convey us to half-time.

Then Ayr winger Jamie Murphy struck the ball against the same section of advertising hoarding two or three times. It appeared as if he was in some kind of pinball point scoring game with himself. The whistle blew, a PA announcer – wearing golden shoes as if after the match he had a gig at a local cabaret club – read the scores from elsewhere and above the floodlights, the moon arrived.

The second half began with Balmoor now glowing against a coal-black sky. Ultra drum thuds competed with the smashing of long balls and the putting of passes. In the main stand, an old man gestured towards Peterhead's pogoing young 'uns and remarked, "They're gonna end up with grumpy knees, that lot."

A minute later, his own knees were endangered by goal celebrations. Peterhead's lead transpired from an Ayr mistake. Midway inside his own half, Murphy juggled the ball and it span in the wrong direction, a magician's dove exiting through a window.

His inadvertent pass curved around teammate Frankie Musonda and left Kieran Shanks – anticipating the mistake like a parent stopping a toddler from hitting his head on the side of a table – through on goal. Shanks steadied himself and jabbed the ball into the far corner. Knees groaned in delirium, hardened northerners hurrahed and somewhere out at sea a patchy radio signal had trawlermen whooping. McGeady was substituted to yet more jeers – "Go

The power of the fork. Pre-match at Balmoor Stadium, Peterhead.

The Somerset Ragazzi cheer on Ayr United.

Joy for these Peterhead fans as they take a second-half lead over Ayr.

and collect your pension, son" said the old man. The shock was on; the cup was magic.

Ayr chased the game, with three men sent high to plunder. Time and again, they were repelled by David Wilson, a lesser-spotted low-socked centre-half. One shot slapped against his legs with such velocity that the collision made the sound of a backfiring space shuttle. Co-manager Brown brought himself on and quickly softened the Ayr onslaught with a safe backwards header to goalkeeper Stuart McKenzie. It seemed to boast of responsibility and calm, like a janitor at the back of the assembly hall jangling a cluster of keys.

And then the magic died, cudgelled by a punted cross, a flick on and a lunging finish from the Ayr captain, Sean McGinty. It was the 96th minute. 1-1. Peterhead players raised hands to heads or sank to the turf. The young ultras reassumed their indoor voices. A middle-aged woman nearby fulminated against some unseen, ungiven foul. "Ye bunch of cheats! Nothing's ever fair".

In extra time Peterhead tussled on, but an Ayr winner felt inevitable, as if a mathematician and not a poet was now scripting this tie's end. Ayr's Fraser Bryden was the man to fit the narrative. The substitute patted the ball forwards, a cat toying with a mouse, and shoved the ball home.

It was not long until the whistle's shrill peep. Ayr United, saluted by their merry band, had stories left to write. Any splash that could be heard was possibly a fisherman's radio landing in the sea. ●

RESULTS:
DUNFERMLINE ATHLETIC 0, RAITH ROVERS 3
PETERHEAD 1, AYR UNITED 2

Flying the flag for Ayr in their 2-1 win over Peterhead.

FOURTH ROUND

FEATURING

FOFAR ATHLETIC V HIBERNIAN
20 January 2024
Station Park

CELTIC V BUCKIE THISTLE
21 January 2024
Celtic Park

The Fourth Round involved a total of 32 clubs from the the Premiership, the Championship, League One, League Two, Highland League and Lowland League

The colours might be the same but these Buckie fans know it will take a miracle to get something against the might of Celtic.

CHAPTER 5

BUCKIE BRING THE TONIC

Our cup hibernated over Christmas and awoke in deepest winter. It was time for minnows to supply the light...

Welcome to Paradise, on a cold and very wet Scottish Cup day in Glasgow.

Why does the cup shock electrify us? It seems impossible to imagine meeting a football fan who says of a tie they are neutral to: "Oh, I hope the bigger team wins." Oddly, beside "underdog" my thesaurus has the synonyms 'loser, victim, scapegoat, fall guy', and yet we see that team as nothing such. The underdog is an heroic outsider, the people's champion, a plucky upstart here to shake the foundations of the game.

It is Robin Hood, David pelting Goliath, Cinderella scoring without her boot on. We revel in their triumph and perhaps even more in their opponent's surprise slaying; watching coverage of any such result, the despairing expressions of the defeated are every bit as attractive and delightful to us as the triumphant salutes of the victorious. The unlikely victory gives us the opposite to a sense of injustice and a rare feeling that sometimes, fairytales happen on muddy fields.

Faded games and grainy goals become part of our personal and shared folklore. Scorelines and the scorers who created them seem to fall into our brains genetically or like times tables and the alphabet. Sometimes, they relate to miracles that erupted before we were even born.

We know 1967 and Jock Wallace's Berwick Rangers beating the other Rangers 1-0. We can't remember our godparents' names but we recall instantly that of Adrian Sprott, and his hitherto hapless Hamilton downing Rangers again. There too might be useless Cowdenbeath, physically allergic to winning football matches, defeating Partick Thistle in '93. Soon afterwards, as if this all happened on the same heavenly day, we see Terry Christie in his coat and Aberdeen pilfered 2-0 at Ochilview. Celts come into view – Inverness Caley making headlines, Clyde riling Roy Keane.

But then the magic died? Not a chance. Your grandkids will remember Brora flogging Hearts and Kelty trampling the holders. Someone else's grandkids may even be named Darvel. These are vintage times for Cinderella and Robin Hood, and so we trekked to Station Park and green Glasgow in search of underdogs with wagging tails.

Forfar failed us, though deserved more from their Saturday afternoon fling with Hibernian. So it was that on a sodden Sunday those of us with no Hoops to wear looked hopefully to Parkhead. Travelling 200 miles south were

> **Around 30 coaches had trudged south, clingfilmed rolls crinkling and flask coffee peppering the air. There would be 3,000 Jags fans at Celtic Park, one third of Buckie's population.**

Buckie Thistle of the Highland League. Even a mere draw would constitute a giant killing on a scale unseen since Jack took his junior hacksaw to the beanstalk. Bookies' Buckie odds of 100/1 seemed miserly. No matter the result, they would earn club-changing sums of up to £250,000.

Around 30 coaches had trudged south, clingfilmed rolls crinkling and flask coffee peppering the air. There would be 3,000 Jags fans at Celtic Park, one third of Buckie's population. Such numbers as these enrich the cup tie every bit as much as stories of bakeries cooking special cakes in the local team's colours or supporters travelling thousands of miles for their club's Big Day Out. Even allowing for exiles in the Parkhead Buckie enclosure who had not travelled from the north-east, the idea that almost one third of a place's residents were attending an away fixture mattered. It is hard to think of any other pastime that could trigger such a migration. A Cup does this to people.

Missing from the 3,000 would be Buckie Thistle's most famous fan. Four years previously, the great American novelist Stephen King had been searching a list of teams for a character in his novel If It Bleeds to follow. He was struck by the Jags' "gorgeous name" and romance bloomed. A shirt and scarf went to America, signed books by return post to the Moray Firth. There were, though, no Greyhound coaches from Maine to Parkhead that Sunday. "Best of success," King had said in a message, "Go Buckies. Show the Celtics how to play the game." One of King's follow-ups to If It Bleeds, incidentally, was titled Fairy Tale.

His team arrived, stepping from their bus looking part professional and part awestruck. To know you are living in a day you will always

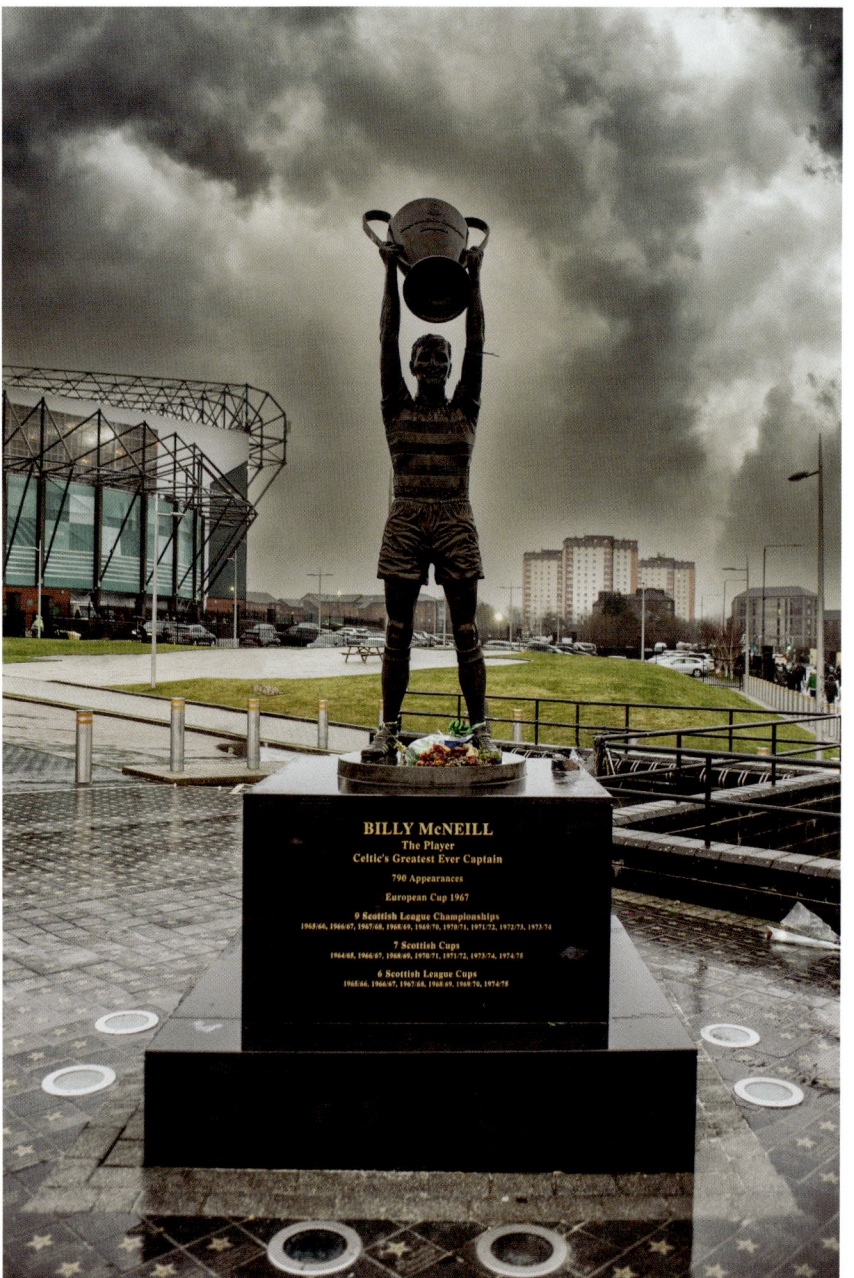

Above: Despite the gathering clouds, the statue of Billy McNeill lifting the European Cup still proclaims Celtic's finest hour.

Right: Scarves are always needed but umbrellas would be more useful on this wet day in Glasgow's East End.

Chapter 5 | **Cup Tied** | 91

Former Celtic manager Neil Lennon poses for a selfie before the fourth round Scottish Cup match.

> **They cheered the warm-up and were near delirious to witness men they knew from work or the pub skimming aimless passes across the hallowed turf.**

remember is a privilege of humanity, albeit a rare one.

Beneath clouds of concrete candyfloss, the coach convoy meandered down London Road. Tourist passengers emerged into the gloom, greeted by a steely gale just as a gust of warm air salutes summer travellers to Spain. On the merchandise stalls, scarves jolted violently like the angry tentacles of some rabid sea beast. "This Is Paradise" announced huge lettering clamped to the Main Stand. I would've asked for my money back.

Holding tight their hats and hoods, though, visitors glanced up to the statue of Jinky Johnstone and grinned. "This is a wee bit different to Keith," said one of them. Presumably he meant Buckie's local rivals Keith FC, or otherwise just a friend named Keith who didn't look like the statue.

Inside the ground, the Buckie boys and girls had found their seats early, though most stood. They cheered the warm-up and were near delirious to witness men they knew from work or the pub skimming aimless passes across the hallowed turf. Fierce rain stabbed at floodlight bulbs but they could not imagine being anywhere else on earth.

Celtic rested few first teamers and started the game with a scorn for fairytales, clipping the ball around with zeal. The Jags, though, were resolute and occasionally bold. It took 20 minutes for Celtic to breach the barricade, though that one was disallowed. Twice more over the afternoon their goals would be discounted; at least the assistant referee's flag had a sense of romance.

Yet soon the Celts plundered bona fide goals. First dancing Matt O'Riley dissected northern resistance with a handsome pass and Paulo Bernado chipped home. Norwegian Odin Thiago Holm – with a preference for bloody sagas over the Disney saccharine perhaps – doubled the lead, a putted finish in off the post.

Then, just before half-time, a moment that had the coachloads screeching in the rain: Buckie forward Josh Peters hauled himself through on goal. Peters saw the net. Peters saw the headlines. Peters saw Joe Hart save with his legs. One day, young doe-eyed members of the Peters family will hear the words, "Did I ever tell you about the time I nearly scored against Joe Hart? He was the England keeper, you know..." A minute later Kyogo Furuhashi had made it 3-0 after intricate work from Liel Abada. How this game turns in the time it takes for a raindrop to fall from a cloud to the turf.

After half-time, 4-0 took the shape of a Luis Palma strike from the edge of the area, and five a first goal for young Rocco Vata after Mikey Johnston conjured and teased. In-between, Peters menaced again, riling Liam Scales into some rough and tumble in the penalty area. Surely a consoling penalty in front of the Moray travellers? VAR does not, though, deal in magic. It is the child who reads manuals and textbooks instead of ghost stories and yarns about people who could fly. No pen.

Celtic manufactured more chances as Buckie tired. In their goal Stuart Knight saved them all, soaring across his goal like, well, Peter Pan in shinpads. Now the rain stopped and the wind cackled. Not at Buckie, though; they had done themselves proud and earned well. Their receipts would, it later emerged, be spent on a new drainage system at their home ground. The glamour of it all. ●

RESULTS:
CELTIC 5, BUCKIE THISTLE 0
FORFAR ATHLETIC 0, HIBERNIAN 1

Hot food on a cold day from a metro-tiled snack bar at Celtic Park.

Chapter 5 | **Cup Tied** | 93

A long way from the bright lights of Leith Walk. Hibs fans wait for entry against the backdrop of Angus farmland.

Ready for kick-off on a grey January day as Forfar host Hibs.

Chapter 5 | **Cup Tied** | 95

It would be rude not to – Hibs fans ponder their choice of Forfar Bridies en-route to the match.

Club officials make their way in to Forfar's Station Park.

Chapter 5 | Cup Tied | 97

Don't worry if you missed the Bridie Shop in town – plenty more available inside the ground.

Darkness falls but Hibs fans are happy enough with a 1-0 win.

The Fultras, The Forfar Ultras, or the Looooonie Army.

Forfar's Josh Skelly takes on Paul Hanlon of Hibs in the Scottish Cup fourth round tie.

FIFTH ROUND

FEATURING

GREENOCK MORTON V MOTHERWELL
9 February 2024
Cappielow Park

ABERDEEN V BONNYRIGG ROSE
10 February 2024
Pittodrie Stadium

The Fifth Round involved a total of 16 clubs from the Premiership, the Championship, League One and League Two

Not even the February Friday night rain can keep the faithful away from the Morton v Motherwell fifth round clash.

The Bois of Motherwell losing attention with their team 2-1 down to Greenock Morton.

CHAPTER 6

FRIDAY I'M IN LOVE

In two grand old theatres of football – Cappielow and Pittodrie – we greedily chased more underdog stories.

Four merrymen of Motherwell sat chatting on a train. As it clattered west towards Greenock, they fell into the usual idle gossip. "He's from Shetland, he lives in Coatbridge but he supports the Accies," said one of a work colleague. "Christ, what must that do to a man?" replied another.

Our Friday evening carriage was perfumed by the rising aromas of chippy suppers. "It's hard with night games, you don't know when to eat," one of the men said. "And you have to leave room for a pie." They nodded along reverently and seriously, as if he were a professor who had just made a salient point about Georgian church architecture. Around us newly opened lager cans hissed and hard raindrops rasped against the windows. "I don't think I can remember a longer winter," said one of the merrymen.

Somewhere after Port Glasgow, Motherwell supporters began to out sing the rain. There was a pause while one of them loudly read out tonight's team, each player cheered. The train shuffled by floodlit Cappielow and its illuminous pitch, a magnificent surprise among the grim black night. It was immediately uplifting, like spotting a fairground in childhood. "Boooooo" responded a number of Steelmen as we passed. "Shitehole."

Trudging through the night around the back of the Wee Dublin End, more Motherwell noise was rising. As ever, walking outside a ground and hearing din from within sparked a strange kind of jealousy, that feeling of being late to a fine party. At the club shop – a truck with a hatch and an orderly bounty – a dad bought his son of four or five a scarf. He looped it around his neck, tied it lovingly tight and patted the boy on the head. Not a word was said but even in the dark it was possible to see the sparks of a journey beginning. In those blue and white bar stripes could be mapped an entire future. It was a far more accurate predictor than any school test. They turned and hand in hand joined a long turnstile queue.

At these moments before an occasion like this, you can *hear* anticipation. Conversation is livelier and more escapist than before a regular league game – it brims with possibility. Rationalism has died a quiet death and now in

Celebrations at Cappielow as Greenock Morton knock Motherwell out of the cup.

Summoned by lights – although you'll have to get past four men and a bin to get inside.

bold terms there is talk of how the lower division team can easily beat their elevated visitors. The mood is higher than it is for a regular league game. There is the sense that this might in the future form one of the "good old days" that will be spoken about in tones of reverence.

It helped that tonight, Cappielow already looked like a fond memory. Floodlights amplified the ground's vintage prowess from the noble main stand to the bustling Cow Shed terrace.

Even rain that seemed to hover like a swarm of insects felt fitting rather than irritating, a prop adding authenticity. Granted, the 1,000 or so Motherwell supporters being doused in the open air Wee Dublin End may not have agreed. Still they sang while the boisterous Cow Shed choir pogoed. It was good to see this beautiful museum busy.

The floodlights also wielded their magic on the two teams' shirts. The blue and white hoops of Morton and Motherwell's amber with claret band were radiant, as if painted by some meticulous model hobbyist. This nostalgic climate was enhanced by players on each side having magnificent, comic strip surnames: Strapp, Power, Blues, Gent, Spittal. I thought back to the far flung summer and recalled Race of Loch Ness. The Scottish Cup brings out the cartoon in all of us.

From the start, Morton pestered the Steelmen and then used possession far better than them, passing crisply and precisely as if showing affection to the ball. There were early free-kicks that threatened the Motherwell goal, although one floated away from danger on the wind like a frisbee on a beach. Ton forward George Oakley rattled the bar. Visiting keeper Liam Kelly docked a goal kick in the home team dugout prompting encouraging roars from home supporters as such errors always do. "Mon eh Toooonnnnn" cried a man behind me. It sounded as though he had mistakenly hit his thumbnail with a hammer, but was in fact a howl of support.

Carried by the breeze, a black dog waste bag pursued the Motherwell right-back, Stephen O'Donnell, who was oblivious to this unorthodox

man-marking job. The scene artfully reflected his team's weak first-half display, which seemed more like a collective shrug of the shoulders than anything containing tactical nutrition.

Then details of a car were read from the Tannoy, its owner encouraged to move it. We as supporters never do get to know if these situations are resolved; perhaps there should be an update in the following game's match programme. Soon afterwards came another such request, this time for the owner of a bus to return to his or her vehicle. Hope sprang that this was now a pattern and increasingly large vehicles would be announced until the pilot of a Boeing 737 walked sheepishly in front of the Cow Shed, keys in hand.

Encouraged by the endeavour of swaggering left-back Lewis Strapp, Morton pushed on, hitting the bar and forcing more corners. Noise from the home terraces gathered and swirled. In the main stand fans banged their feet on the wooden floors. It felt suddenly as if football had never really changed. And then their Morton team scored with a scrambled effort that winced and croaked over the line.

Above: Morton celebrate their second against Motherwell after a George Oakley goal.

Right: YES YA DANCER! Morton score a second against Motherwell.

It was eventually declared an own goal from Motherwell's Harry Paton, a bewildered Canadian who had possibly never seen anything like Cappielow before. Goalkeeper Kelly wore the look of a man who had been locked out of the house in his pyjamas. The rain thickened to resemble signal interference on an old television. Here, now, was a cup tie. The half-time whistle peeped – Greenockians cheered as if shipbuilding had returned to the port; Steelmen bawled and booed as if inebriated at a pantomime.

At the start of the second half, the rain stopped. It was an improbable occurrence up there with the parting of the seas or encountering a clean table in a Wetherspoons pub. A gaggle of Morton fans migrated from the Cow Shed to the open

Motherwell put Morton under late pressure but it is not enough and the home team hold on for a 2-1 victory at Cappielow.

> **At the start of the second half, the rain stopped. It was an improbable occurrence up there with the parting of the seas or encountering a clean table in a Wetherspoons pub.**

Empty spaces at the Motherwell end as their team go down 2-1 to Morton.

terrace at one end, hoping to entice a second goal. It worked. Oakley rampaged through and from the edge of the penalty area pummelled a shot into the far corner of Kelly's domain. The ball span dizzily on impact with the net, a snared animal. Cappielow erupted and for older followers in their wizened scarves time blurred – this was how the old place used to sound when Andy Ritchie was conjuring his magic.

Motherwell boss Stuart Kettlewell responded by making a triple substitution, the managerial equivalent of sending misbehaving kids to stand in a corner of the classroom facing the wall. His side at last gathered some momentum, but it was more traction engine than bullet train. One shot soared high and wide as if the ball was attempting to flee and claim asylum in Dunoon.

Morton continued to thrive, powering through with heart and guile. "You are my Morton," sang the Cow Shed besotted, "My only Morton…" Victory felt close, the scent of a favourite meal wafting down the hallway. Then, somehow, with five minutes to go Motherwell scored, Jack Vale's tapped shot deflecting in. Hope spread across the Wee Dublin End.

Now came an onslaught, Motherwell scrapping for their Cup place. They were repelled mightily by Morton, whose defenders jumped in front of the ball as if it were a vicious intruder. Soon, fingers visited lips and whistles pierced the air from the Cow Shed to the Main Stand, sending wild instructions to sheepdogs across the water in the Trossachs. Smashed clearances induced heartfelt roars.

From somewhere beneath the cacophony, the referee ended the match. This weathered, gorgeous old ground was drenched in jubilant uproar. As if the scene were unfolding in Hollywood and not Inverclyde, fireworks exploded above us. Finally, we had a Cup shock. If you wore blue and white, these truly were the good old days. ●

RESULTS:
GREENOCK MORTON 2, MOTHERWELL 1
ABERDEEN 2, BONNYRIGG ROSE 0

In LA they'd be the Bleacher seats but not much danger of sunstroke in Aberdeen in February.

Miovski scores his, and Aberdeen's, second to see off Bonnyrigg Rose in the fifth round cup tie at Pittodrie.

"Well done sir!" Miovski gets the plaudits for his two goals from his teammates.

Chapter 6 | **Cup Tied** | 113

The statue of Sir Alex Ferguson reminds Aberdonians of the glory years of the 1980s.

Even on a dreich February afternoon, Pittodrie Stadium radiates old-school charm.

Soul, Spirit and Tradition even on the darkest Aberdeen days.

The hulking, ugly beauty of the Richard Donald stand at Pittodrie.

CHAPTER 7

QUARTER-FINALS

FEATURING

ABERDEEN V KILMARNOCK
9 March 2024
Pittodrie Stadium

HIBERNIAN V RANGERS
10 March 2024
Easter Road

The Quarter-Finals involved a total of 8 clubs from the Premiership and the Championship

118 | Cup Tied

Rangers fans are marshalled toward the away stand at Hibs' Easter Road Stadium.

CHAPTER 7

NORTH SEA BLUES

As western teams travelled eastwards to coastal homes, only eight clubs remained. Daydreams of past glories inspired hopes of May delight.

The windows of the Persevere pub had steamed up so that those inside looked as if they were sitting in a faded photograph. A man threw open the main door to step out for a cigarette and for a moment pre-match hubbub leaked out and cheered the cold air. In this electric hour before kick-off, football drinkers' voices are always buoyant and optimism blooms with every sip.

The mood was heightened by the colours they wore; in 2016, Hibernian fans fell in love with the Scottish Cup all over again. Even eight years on, green eyes still twinkled when their owners thought of that handsome trophy.

It was late afternoon on Mother's Day. Cards had been opened, novelty chocolate saved for later and lunches savoured. Now, many mums lifted their scarves from restaurant coat hooks and headed for the match. Whether today's game would represent a treat was not really up to them. Clouds groaned and rain spattered. In the tenement windows of Easter Road, living room lights had been switched on not long after 3pm. Spring seemed more remote than Neptune. "Don't say I'm no good to you" said a man in his forties outside the Famous Five Stand. Inside, an electronic hoarding cheerily bought into the spirit of the day. "Have your funeral with us at Easter Road from £1875."

Not long after the game had started, a Hibernian backpass escaped from the pitch for a Rangers corner. Two tiers of travelling supporters roared with delight. There is in this game so much encouragement to take from the mistakes of others. It came to nothing, and soon Hibs had a corner of their own to fritter. Quickly, and for a good 15 or 20 minutes, the match melted into a formless blob of a spectacle, scratty and shapeless. Rather than engage with the stupor presently unfolding, home fans dreamed themselves eight years back in time to

Pre-match merch before the Hibs-Rangers Quarter-Final match.

Rangers fans crossing the Crawford Bridge en-route to Easter Road.

Hampden. "When the Hibs went up to lift the Scottish Cup/We were there," they sang.

Then Rangers goalkeeper Jack Butland indulged in an act of charity to awaken us all. He had been casually passing the ball around his own penalty area when it became entangled between his feet, a yapping and unshakeable Chihuahua. Hibs' Myziane Maolida chased, lunged and forced a near-goal line shot against the post. The Englishman looked surprised by Maolida's exertion and impudence, as if he were a child whose father had suddenly started going full pelt during a play fight. Today was Butland's birthday which he perhaps presumed brought him some kind of immunity from anything bad happening.

Hibs now stirred, driven largely by the sprightly Joe Newell. If, before, they had been snoozing following a heavy Sunday roast, he was the family member suggesting a brisk stroll. Newell brought order to the home midfield, rolling into a neat sphere the unkempt, unravelled ball of wool it had previously been. Home fans sang for the present rather than the past. Then, perhaps inevitably if you know anything about Hibernian Football Club, their team conceded a penalty against the run of play.

There was no cruelty in Jordan Obita's challenge on Dujon Sterling. The Rangers winger skipped into the area and the chasing Hibee seemed to tread on his heels; they resembled nothing more than kids dashing to take a play park's last free swing. This clumsy

Pre-match ticket pick up at Easter Road.

rather than callous act meant the sparking of protests from team and terrace, but the kick stood. James Tavernier placed the ball down, stepped backwards, performed a quick shuffle waltz and then shot. David Marshall saved easily. Now home fans briefly danced and the ball too gyrated. There was, for them, misfortune in its manoeuvres; it floated to John Lundstram who jabbed the ball in. Elation had passed between the two sets of supporters inside two seconds, a sonic transfer. Leith had awoken.

Rangers, though, possessed a sedative. Their unceasing possession of the ball silenced the home crowd, hypnotism through monotony. Then a hideous North Sea wind recently returned from an Arctic holiday swept across the ground, slapping cheeks and making cosy Mother's Day meals a distant memory. When Hibs did manage to occupy the ball, in their forward play they resembled cats in sludge. Then Martin Boyle, their regular inspiration, was stretchered off injured. As he writhed on the floor, it felt as though the temperature had dropped further. Hope dwindled. Soon afterwards, the half-time whistle prompted home jeering for the referee, Hibs' flimsy attacking play and the very concept of being inside a numbing football ground and not in the pub.

Stimulated by the verve of Boyle's replacement Élie Youan, their team embarked on another energetic burst at the beginning of the second half, plundering a series of corners. These phases of sudden Hibs activity brought to mind a drunk

Supporters mill around outside the Main Stand at Easter Road.

> **VAR examined the Moriah-Welsh red while he stood on the touchline, a condemned man with a reprieve dangled, and then quashed. Down the tunnel he trudged.**

passing between phases of comatose sleep and vivid conversation.

True to that template, they were soon engaging in clumsy violence. First of all, Obita's wrist brushed against Rabbi Matondo's face and the Rangers man fell theatrically. It was enough to warrant a second yellow card for Obita. Then, not three minutes later, Hibs' Nathan Moriah-Welsh scythed through Lundstram, a combine harvester threshing wheat. They would play for the last 20 minutes with nine men. The challenge took place not 10 metres from Obita's indiscretion, in front of the dug outs. It was as if there were some temporary Bermuda Triangle wasting Hibs players. VAR examined the Moriah-Welsh red while he stood on the touchline, a condemned man with a reprieve dangled, and then quashed. Down the tunnel he trudged.

If that killed the tie, Rangers' second goal – an elegant effort from Fábio Silva – buried it in an unmarked grave. Hibs fans left in their thousands, mums included. There were five minutes of futile injury time and those of us that remained in Hibernian sections of the ground felt as if we were the last customers in a shop at closing time, staff sweeping around our feet.

Back behind the steaming windows of the Persevere, analysis lasted for a pint or two and then topics drifted elsewhere. Followers of football move on quickly, because there is always next week, always next year. ●

RESULTS:
ABERDEEN 3, KILMARNOCK 1
HIBERNIAN 0, RANGERS 2

Chapter 7 | Cup Tied | 125

Outside the Famous Five stand before the Hibs–Rangers Quarter-Final tie.

Rangers fans heading to the match.

The Burghead Loyal take their places for the game.

Hibs are inches away from taking the lead against Rangers.

Hibs press Rangers in a rain-soaked Scottish Cup quarter-final clash.

Rangers push forward in their 2-0 away victory over Hibs.

Jubilation as Rangers take the lead at Easter Road.

Rangers fans celebrate as they see off Hibs in a bad-tempered quarter-final tie.

Chapter 7 | **Cup Tied** | 131

Pittodrie begins to fill up for the cup quarter-final against Kilmarnock.

Chapter 7 | **Cup Tied** | 133

Fans take their seats early for the Aberdeen v Kilmarnock quarter-final tie.

Kilmarnock fans anxiously watch on as their team take on Aberdeen at Pittodrie.

Chapter 7 | **Cup Tied** | 135

Kilmarnock fans before their clash with Aberdeen.

All smiles before the match.

The long drive is temporarily worth it as Kilmarnock fans celebrate their team pulling a goal back.

Danny Armstrong of Kilmarnock tussles with Aberdeen's Jack MacKenzie.

The old-school Pittodrie floodlights brighten a dull day in Aberdeen.

Celebrations for Aberdeen's second goal of the match.

It's a third for Aberdeen as they book their semi-final place.

Neil Warnock leaves the pitch at the end of the match. He will resign as Aberdeen manager minutes later.

Red Sails. Flag day at Pittodrie.

SEMI FINALS

FEATURING

ABERDEEN V CELTIC
20 April 2024
Hampden Park

RANGERS V HEART OF MIDLOTHIAN
21 April 2024
Hampden Park

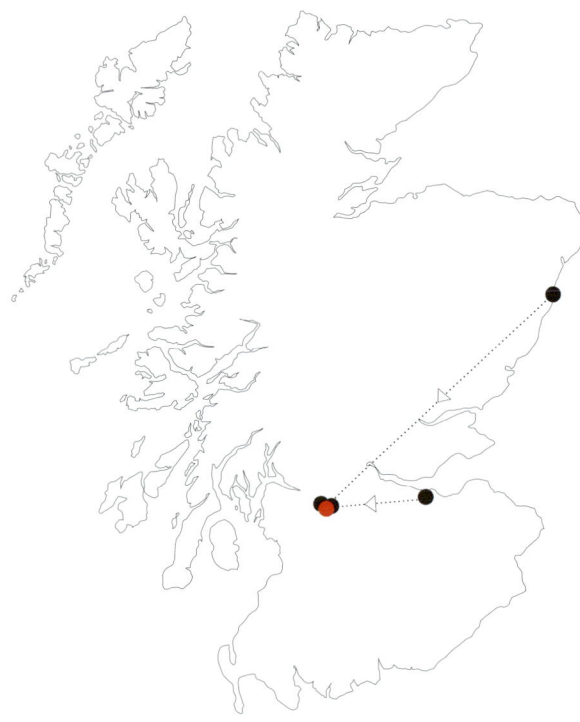

The Semi-Finals involved a total of four clubs from the Premiership

Rangers supporters shelter from the rain outside the West Stand at Hampden Park before the semi-final against Hearts.

CHAPTER 8

THE HAMPDEN FOUR

On an April weekend, troubled Dons and buoyant Jambos trek to Hampden. Greens and Blues await them, determined to concoct a first Old Firm final in two decades.

A Railway Bear outside Hampden Park.

There were three of them, now inhabiting a nightmare. An anxiety dream of the type we have all had in the earliest hours of a matchday had become real.

There are variations to this infiltrated sleep: sometimes, it is Saturday, 2pm and we are hundreds of miles from the ground, frantically pacing the streets of Exeter when we need to be in Montrose; or, a rogue coach driver is speeding us further and further away from the stadium. Later we awake, relieved. In real life we always make kick-off.

Here, now, in the very solid and conscious world of a Scotrail carriage, one of the trio had asked a question: "Jamie, have you got the tickets?" It was nearing 1pm. They had boarded at Haymarket, bound for Hampden to watch Hearts, late because one them had slept in. "No," said Jamie, "Why is it always my job?" The other two didn't believe him, thought he was joking; then they half-believed him, and then a sort of jovial doom of realisation engulfed them all.

Three tickets for the Scottish Cup semi-final really were lying abandoned on the kitchen table. "How is it my fault!?" asked Jamie.

Frantically, just as in one of those nightmares, they hatched plans involving a train back to Edinburgh, a taxi, another train, another taxi. "Fuck it," one of the three said as they alighted at Linlithgow, "Rangers are gonna gub us anyhow. Let's just go to the pub." "We should at least try," said Jamie, inhabiting the frenzied spirit of that supporter in dreamland. "And at least we can get train cans now."

The train pushed on without them, and another heaved us towards Hampden. It clattered through suburban Glasgow's hushed Sunday and delivered us into a fizzing, vivid community: that of an Occasion. A Cup that started out in routine matchdays had now been honed and refined into limited edition fixtures. This was a drama, an event. It showed in the way

Hearts fans begin to arrive at the East Stand for the Scottish Cup semi-final against Rangers.

> **The sight of two illegally parked cars being hauled onto a removal truck contrived to heighten the buoyant mood. Schadenfreude as a pre-match ritual.**

men and women in maroon strutted towards the stadium, their children and grandchildren begging for a special scarf or souvenir programme or ice cream from the Mister Softee van, or all three. The sight of two illegally parked cars being hauled onto a removal truck contrived to heighten the buoyant mood. Schadenfreude as a pre-match ritual.

There was even something sprightlier in the trots of Hampden-weary Rangers supporters as they vaulted steps towards turnstiles. Then came those markers of all big games: lone men stood holding single match tickets in the air, Statues of Liberty offering a seat behind the goal for 30 quid.

Beside the radiant Hampden turf, fans applauded their players as they finished warming up and returned to the changing room, another hallmark of an Occasion. There is no such time to spare before humdrum league fixtures when a quick last pint can be swilled. Soon, the two teams had returned to thunder from the terraces, both ends corralled by groups in black, the Gorgie Ultras and the Union Bears. They had much to live up to. Perhaps too much, in fact. A humdinger of a semi-final the previous day had seen Celtic defeat intrepid, unlucky Aberdeen on penalties after a three-all draw. Being on the pitch now already felt like recording a difficult second album.

Referee Steven McLean counted his 22 men like a nervous shepherd and 20,000 Hearts fans twirled their scarves, a riot of static. They believed. This could happen. It was already possible to imagine an open top bus parade on Gorgie Road. There were even balloons. And then Cyriel Dessers danced loose in the box and made it 1-0. The blue half of the ground was electrified, the maroon barely candlelit. Few pursuits can turn a human from feverish hope to forlorn silence so quickly. The din of those celebrating Gers boxed their ears. "Nice one, Cyriel" they sang, dusting down and reprising a 1970s classic dedicated to Spurs full-back Cyril Knowles. Down in front of me, a man wearing a Hearts scarf tried to stamp a balloon to death but succeeded only in falling over.

For a good while Rangers dominated. They were often orchestrated by John Lundstram, a methodical, textbook footballer who on the ball seems to move predictably yet effectively through a process, as if showing his workings: check, receive, kill ball, check again, simple pass. At one point, however, he skimmed a ball 40 yards across the pitch. It whizzed beyond players from both teams. They watched the Size 5 as if admiring a decent frisbee throw in the local park. It absconded from play and landed at the feet of Hearts manager Steven Naismith. This occurrence seemed more like a system malfunction than a mistake. I half expected to see James Tavernier, the Rangers skipper, switch Lundstram off and then on again.

Then Hearts' own lynchpin, Beni Baningime, helped his frenetic side find rhythm and belief. Lawrence Shankland – who in Knowles' 1970s would have been described as a "chunky raider" – scooped in a cross. Full-back Frankie Kent arrived in the six-yard box with impeccable timing to greet it. He stretched a leg and poked the ball. Surely a goal. He too could imagine the Gorgie bus parade. Miraculously Jack Butland perfectly executed an airborne crab football manoeuvre to save with his feet.

As the second half began, clouds cracked and the sun shone. The oval of sky above us was now a chirpy blue, reminding us that the football season was scampering towards its resolutions and heartbreaks. A ball boy dribbled his allotted charge through a trackside puddle deposited by earlier rain. He looked across to the pitch and, you hope, dreamed of being on the other side of the touchline. What is this game for if not such heady hallucinations?

Hearts' Alan Forrest – his socks lowering as the match progressed as if performing a niche form of striptease – repeatedly nipped and connived his way through opponents. His trickery had maroon scarves twirling again. Shankland ruffled blue feathers, a nuisance neighbour. All accompanying music was sung in Gorgie tones. When the ball moved closer to Butland's goal, eager, anticipating sounds grew

Hot snacks on a cold day. Up the steps to the Rangers End at Hampden.

> **When the ball moved closer to Butland's goal, eager, anticipating sounds grew as they always do when supporters feel they can see a few seconds into the future.**

Pre-match fuelling up for Hearts fans at the Sportsmans. A foot long sausage on offer.

as they always do when supporters feel they can see a few seconds into the future.

Yet every Hearts attack fizzled to nought when the goalframe was in sight. It brought to mind being a teenager and watching friends approaching girls they had a crush on but then asking them for the time or whether they'd done their maths homework. Even worse, a Shankland header hit the side netting, meaning half the Jambos fans erupted in glee before realising they were mistaken – here's what you could've won.

Not long afterwards, Todd Cantwell whirled his way through a Hearts backline emaciated by the chase for an equaliser. He jabbed the ball to Dessers. Craig Gordon staved off his first shot; the net felt the force of his second. Two-nil, and a first Old Firm final in over 20 years could be added to the calendar.

Hearts continued to compete robustly. Refereeing decisions against them provoked in their crowd an ire that was soon replaced by resignation. It was interesting to observe the different moments that prompted their fans to leave. For some, a misplaced Jambos pass induced a dismissive wave of the arm and then a lunge for the exit, head shaking. Others sprang up in indignation against a refereeing decision and jogged up the steps without looking back. A misplaced pass was enough for many, even if they offered fleeting applause in the manner of disappointed gameshow contestants striving to be courteous to a winner.

Presumably somewhere among them, Jamie turned to his two friends and said: "You're right. We should've gone to the pub." ●

RESULTS:
ABERDEEN 3, CELTIC 3
CELTIC WON ON PENALTIES 5-6 AFTER EXTRA TIME
RANGERS 2, HEART OF MIDLOTHIAN 0

All smiles before their semi-final against Rangers.

More smiles from the Rangers fans pre-match. It would be the supporters in blue who were still smiling a couple of hours later.

Chapter 8 | **Cup Tied** | 153

Pre-match confidence from these Celtic fans.

A warm day at Hampden for the Aberdeen v Celtic semi-final.

We all fall down. Fatigue and injury take a toll in the closing stages of Rangers' 2-0 Scottish Cup victory over Hearts.

Cyriel Dessers celebrates his second goal.

The red and the green. Which side are you on?

Ester Sokler scores a late equaliser for Aberdeen to send the match into extra time.

Despite missing his own penalty Joe Hart ends up being the hero as he saves from Killian Phillips in the shootout to send Celtic to the final.

Chapter 8 | **Cup Tied** | 161

THE FINAL

FEATURING
CELTIC V RANGERS
25 May 2024
Hampden Park

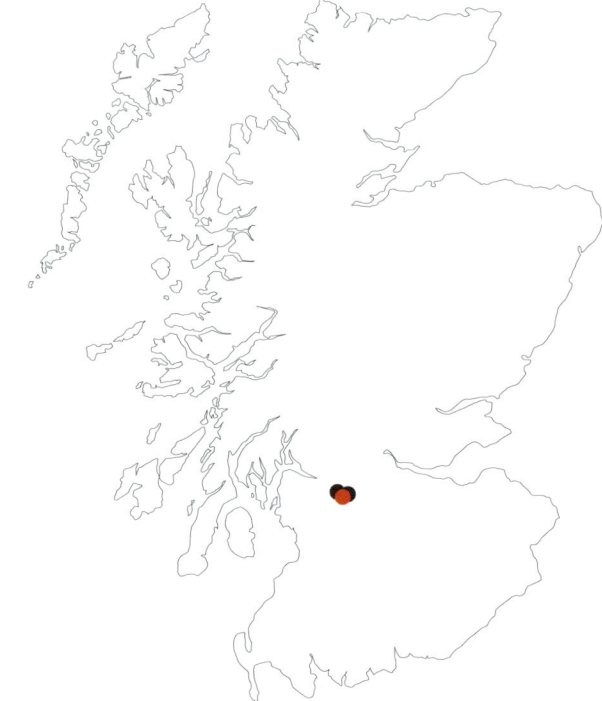

The Final involved two clubs from the Premiership

Which colour ribbons will be tied to the trophy at 4.45?

CHAPTER 9

AND THEN THERE WERE TWO

Over the cup's course, 131 teams had been whittled to two. Now this famous pair restoked their rivalry at Hampden, marking the end of our odyssey.

Smoke from the pre-match pyrotechnics clears to reveal the Celtic huddle before the match.

It was Cup Final Day and yet life proceeded as normal on Buchanan Street. Didn't the howling busker care that the first Old Firm final in 20 odd years would soon be kicking off? Would the man pushing a petition to cease this or start that be putting down his clipboard in time for 3pm?

Then, around a corner, the everyday altered to matchday. With green flags draped across shoulders or blue scarves looped around necks, supporters of Celtic and Rangers now outnumbered plain-clothed civilians. The route to Glasgow Central station was paved with hope. Even bitter enemies such as these shared that much.

From among the scarlet tenement streets of Mount Florida, both tribes emerged and made for their Hampden quarters. They paid men wearing pouches for souvenir scarves and queued to add another programme to the pile. These two clubs may have made Hampden roar more than all others, but a Cup Final would still never bring out the blasé in them. Today mattered, not least because a victory over loathed rivals is richer than any other.

As so often is the case in our minds at least, the sun knew it was Cup Final day. With each minute until the game's start it seemed to burn brighter and breathe more heavily. While thermometer readings soared so too did decibel levels. Ends blue and green unleashed lavish tifo and flag displays. Smoke from the flares they detonated shrouded the pitch and mingled in the centre circle. For a while this concocted pea-souper changed the season from early summer to deepest winter. The haze lingered through Celtic's team huddle, simultaneously cheered riotously and booed rigorously. Gentle Luncarty seemed like a different sport from another time.

The game began chaotically, a stampede. It was like watching news footage of hysterical

> **Players that five minutes ago were fit only for the glue factory were now so many stallions in green and white favours.**

shoppers on Black Friday. Gradually, the two sides agreed upon a loose pattern of play – Celtic's patient attempts to stretch and contort their opponents versus Rangers' more dynamic, direct approach. Both were urged on by their wildly gesticulating managers, Brendan Rodgers and Philippe Clement. They stood in the shade of their technical areas resembling headmasters watching Sports Day.

Neither team much troubled the two goalkeepers, Celtic's Joe Hart in his final ever match and Jack Butland, Rangers' fellow former England international. This inaction did at least give Hart the chance to consider which retirement hobbies to take up. Indeed, now seemed an opportune moment to make a start, and it would not have made much difference had he removed his gloves, set up a trestle table and begun working on an Airfix model Spitfire kit.

Although the energetic Todd Cantwell – his hair flapping like a flannel on a breezy washing line – did his best to enliven the match in Rangers' favour, it still had the barren feeling of a game of chess with no pieces. Some of us wished the pre-match flare fog had loitered and obscured the whole thing. The half-time whistle was a sweet lullaby.

When the game restarted, Rangers found a rhythm. They were conducted by Mohamed Diomande, a man unruffled by the surrounding bedlam. The midfielder's calm provided a base from which those around him could attack. Celtic looked rattled, repeatedly resembling cats

On the Cathcart Road before the Old Firm final.

running from the vacuum cleaner. When they did capture the ball, they exasperated their crowd by dawdling or passing it straight out of play.

With an hour played, Rangers' dominance won them a corner. James Tavernier lifted the kick so that it eluded Hart and several Celtic men at the near post. The ball then fell like a can plummeting from a vending machine onto the knee of Gers substitute Abdallah Sima, and popped into the net. Blue delirium followed. So did a VAR check. Rangers fans were still in heaven when the ruling came: no goal. There had apparently been a foul on Hart. The big screen was a telegram bringing bad news from the frontline. A joyous moment had been repealed. The goal was a lie. Celtic fans now rejoiced.

The annulment boosted their team, though Rangers continued to push forward more convincingly. They won a trio of fruitless corners in quick succession. Celtic continued to make mistakes and appeared flustered. Hart hoisted a clearance straight out of play and several players made passes to ghosts no-one else could see. A great cloud of grumbles gathered. Impending extra time loomed like a late shift.

Eighty-nine minutes had passed when Celtic's Paulo Bernardo received the ball in the centre circle. He hopscotched around a challenge from Nicolas Raskin and dashed 30 yards unhindered. From the edge of the D, Bernardo clipped in a shot. Butland saw the diving catch coming his way and the counter-attack he could spring. His hands disagreed.

The goalkeeper padded uncertainly at the ball, a man on holiday palming off a local delicacy he didn't wish to eat. He flopped forward to rescue the danger. Celtic's Adam Idah got there first. The striker jabbed the ball into the net. Hooped shirts uncoiled in frantic revelry. Words and sentences could never capture the ecstasy of a last-minute cup final winner against acidic rivals. It fired emotions beyond explanation or comprehension. Only euphoric yowls would do.

How they cheered their team through injury time. Players that five minutes ago were fit only for the glue factory were now so many stallions in green and white favours. Celtic fans pogoed and worked through a set list of anthems. Every Rangers follower looked like the victim of a pickpocketing. The full-time whistle was both a pardon and a death sentence.

Soon one half of Hampden was barren and the other boisterous. Fireworks popped and golden ticker tape flickered. The old trophy's ribbons matched green and white threads now held aloft.

They sang 'You'll Never Walk Alone'. Watching the Scottish Cup in its birthday season, we hadn't. We had joined the thousands whose weekend plans had been sparked by the evocative words: "And that concludes the draw…" We had stood in their charming rickety homes in the autumn and sat in luscious Mount Florida in May. We had marvelled as early rounds of teams called Lily, Bluebell and Rose flowered into terrace choristers and players smooching medals. We had seen how this competition is still club-coloured cakes in the town bakery and first-timers next to old-timers behind the goal, all of them jolted to joy when a volley kisses the net.

The Scottish Cup is a constant. It is chiselled in silver and engraved on a nation. The magic remains intact. ●

RESULT:
CELTIC 1, RANGERS 0

No pre-match nerves before the big match..

No cup final is complete without a home-made trophy.

Pre-match confidence is high before the game.

All quiet before the game but VAR would play a big part later in the match.

The kits for the match officials.

Allez les blues! Rangers fans cheer on their team.

Top: Dujon Sterling powers goalward from out wide. Bottom: Abdallah Sima holds off Celtic's Liam Scales.

Chapter 9 | **Cup Tied** | 173

It could have been so different. Abdallah Sima's goal is soon chalked off for a push on Joe Hart in the Celtic goal.

VAR breaks the Rangers fan's hearts.

Adam Idah celebrates his last minute cup final winner in front of a rapturous Celtic support.

Alistair Johnston, Greg Taylor and Joe Hart take a moment before going up to collect the cup.

Callum McGregor and Joe Hart lift the cup together as Celtic celebrate the double.

The class of '24 as Celtic celebrate winning the cup in the 150th anniversary final.

Callum McGregor enjoying the moment as he captain Celtic to the cup.

Chapter 9 | **Cup Tied** | 181

SOMETHING IN THE AIR

Finals of the Scottish Cup have been played at nine different venues. Here, aerial shots of those existent and demolished give a unique perspective.

CHAPTER 10

Does football leave footprints? Can you tell where it once lived? Certainly, those whose teams have left beloved homes can. One walks over the retail park tarmac which heinously replaced his team's old ground and pictures the penalty spot. Another strolls through the housing estate layered over her's and swears she can smell frying hot dog onions and hear the calls of programme sellers. These are sacred sites. There is something different about them. Football woz 'ere.

The same might not be true for the bulldozed football places none of us knew. It is hard as you roar over the M8 to imagine a goalmouth where a lorry now rolls, difficult to picture a club house in the middle lane. And, it is unlikely that those who live in the flats where the first Cathkin Park dwelled know to look for ghosts of moustachioed goalkeepers in the kitchen or outside rights darting through the living room.

This forgetting makes remembering through photos and maps important. It marks these places' existences and summons their spirits. It uncovers the venues where goals were scored, trophies lifted and greatest days revelled in.

We can also see here living, breathing current homes of football, only differently. Here they are in the context of their surroundings; communities within others.

After much marauding, the Scottish Cup found its way home. These photos are a record of how it got there. ●

The three Hampdens. The location of the original Hampden Park is to the right with the second Hampden Park (which became New Cathkin Park) in the foreground and the third and current Hampden Park in the top left.

Where it all began. The original Hampden Park was the home ground of Queen's Park from 1873 to 1883 and also hosted numerous international matches with Scotland thrashing England a regular occurrence. The precise location of the pitch was unknown for years as the ground did not appear on any Ordnance Survey maps from the period and it was only recently that the exact location was discovered thanks to a map belonging to the Caledonian Railway Company coming to light. The ground hosted the first ever final 150 years ago with Queen's Park beating Clydesdale 2-0 in 1874. It last staged the final in 1883 before the construction of the Cathcart Branch Railway Line forced Queen's Park to move to the second Hampden in nearby Cathkin Park.

Cathkin Park (site of). Located to the east of Cathcart Road the original Cathkin Park was owned by Third Lanark and, including replays, hosted the cup final five times between 1880 and 1886. Third Lanark would move on to New Cathkin Park after Queen's Park built the third Hampden in 1903.

Kinning Park was orginally home to the Clydesdale Cricket Club. In 1872 Clydesdale FC, an offshoot of the cricket club was formed and they were the original football team at the ground. By 1876 both the cricket and the football club had moved on to Titwood and the ground was taken over by Rangers FC who played at Kinning Park until their move to Ibrox in 1887. Kinning Park hosted the Scottish Cup Final for the only time in 1881. Queen's Park beat Dumbarton 2-1 in front of a crowd of 15000 spectators but the match was declared void after Dumbarton protested that people had strayed on to the pitch. An aggrieved Queen's Park then beat them 3-1 in the rearranged tie. The M8 motorway now runs over the area.

The First Ibrox. The original Ibrox Stadium was slightly to the Northeast of the present stadium and was home to Rangers from 1887 until 1899 when the new and current Ibrox was constructed. The original Ibrox hosted the final seven times (including replays) between 1890 and 1895.

For the only time in the competition's history, the 1896 final was played outside Glasgow. As Hearts and Hibs had reached the final, and Hampden was hosting an international rugby match, it was decided to play the match in Edinburgh and St Bernard's FC ground at New Logie Green was chosen to host. Hearts would go on to beat Hibernian 3-1. The ground lasted until 1899 when St Bernard's moved on, and ultimately housing was developed on the site.

Top left: Celtic Park hosted the final several times in the early twentieth century and has been used occasionally since due to redevelopment at Hampden.
Top right: Ibrox Stadium was the cup final venue several times between 1900 and 1924 but has only been used once since, in 1996, when Kilmarnock defeated Falkirk 1-0.
Bottom left: The Second Hampden. After moving from the original Hampden, the Queen's Park ground first hosted the final in 1885 and continued to do so until 1899. Queen's Park would move to the third (and current) Hampden in 1903 and Third Lanark moved in and renamed the ground New Cathkin Park (later just Cathkin Park).
Bottom right: Hamilton Crescent Cricket Ground is most famous for being the venue for the first ever international match as Scotland drew 0-0 with England in 1872. The ground hosted the Scottish Cup finals of 1876 and 1877 won by Queen's Park and Vale of Leven respectively.

Camelon Juniors ultras, some more interested than others.

Towards the promise of floodlights at Musselburgh.

PRELIMINARY ROUND ONE
12 August 2023
Carnoustie Panmure 1–2 Beith Juniors
CHAPTER 1 → Luncarty 3–1 Loch Ness
Abbey Vale 0–5 Cupar Hearts

PRELIMINARY ROUND TWO
2 September 2023
Beith Juniors 5–1 Bonnyton Thistle
Culter 3–2 Blackburn United
Preston Athletic 0–0 Dundonald Bluebell (a.e.t.) (4–5 pens)
Hill of Beath Hawthorn 0–1 Tayport
Dunbar United 4–2 Vale of Leithen
Carluke Rovers 2–3 Dalbeattie Star (a.e.t.)
Tynecastle 0–1 Hutchison Vale
Jeanfield Swifts 3–0 Cupar Hearts
St Andrews United 1–0 Haddington Athletic
Wigtown & Bladnoch 0–12 Auchinleck Talbot
Irvine Meadow 1–2 Dunipace
CHAPTER 1 → Pollok 2–2 Benburb (a.e.t.) (3–0 pens)
Newton Stewart 1–4 Luncarty
Sauchie Juniors 4–0 Burntisland Shipyard
St Cuthbert Wanderers 0–5 Dalkeith Thistle
Hawick Royal Albert 1–2 Golspie Sutherland
Cumnock Juniors 1–0 Girvan
Creetown 1–3 Whitehill Welfare
Camelon Juniors 0–0 Newtongrange Star (a.e.t.) (4–3 pens)
Easthouses Lily Miners Welfare 1–3 Threave Rovers

Kilwinning Rangers 4–0 Glasgow University
Broxburn Athletic 3–0 Lochee United
Penicuik Athletic 4–2 Rutherglen Glencairn
Glenafton Athletic 0–3 Darvel
Fort William 1–10 Clydebank
Musselburgh Athletic 6–0 Coldstream

FIRST ROUND
23 September 2023
Culter 3–4 Deveronvale (a.e.t.)
Penicuik Athletic 0–6 Pollok
Cowdenbeath 2–1 Linlithgow Rose (a.e.t.)
Clachnacuddin 1–0 Inverurie Loco Works
Dalkeith Thistle 0–7 Clydebank
Formartine United 3–2 Threave Rovers
Dunipace 1–3 Cumnock Juniors (a.e.t.)
Gala Fairydean Rovers 8–2 Strathspey Thistle
Lossiemouth 0–4 Beith Juniors
Wick Academy 1–3 Jeanfield Swifts
Edinburgh University 2–3 Dunbar United
Caledonian Braves 1–2 Fraserburgh
Banks O' Dee 6–0 Dalbeattie Star
Bo'ness United 3–0 Darvel
Turriff United 2–1 Sauchie Juniors
Golspie Sutherland 1–1 Forres Mechanics (a.e.t.) (7–8 pens)
Tayport 0–4 Buckie Thistle
CHAPTER 2 → Camelon Juniors 1–2 Civil Service Strollers
Brechin City 4–0 Rothes
East Stirlingshire 0–1 Huntly

Musselburgh Athletic 1–1 Gretna 2008 (a.e.t.) (4–3 pens)
East Kilbride 8–0 Whitehill Welfare
Keith 2–5 Luncarty
Broxburn Athletic 2–1 Nairn County
Dundonald Bluebell 2–3 Kilwinning Rangers
Brora Rangers 5–1 Berwick Rangers
Tranent 4–1 Hutchison Vale
St Andrews United 1–0 Auchinleck Talbot
Broomhill 3–1 Cumbernauld Colts
CHAPTER 2 → University of Stirling 1–3 Albion Rovers

SECOND ROUND
28 October 2023
Beith Juniors 1–3 Broomhill
Civil Service Strollers 0–3 Stranraer
Albion Rovers 2–1 St Andrews United
Stenhousemuir 0–2 Brora Rangers
Cumnock Juniors 2–1 Turriff United
Kilwinning Rangers 0–1 Cowdenbeath
Peterhead 3–1 Clachnacuddin
Deveronvale 0–1 Broxburn Athletic
Forres Mechanics 0–1 Buckie Thistle
Dumbarton 3–2 Banks O' Dee
Dunbar United 1–0 East Fife
Fraserburgh 1–2 Bonnyrigg Rose (a.e.t.)
CHAPTER 3 → Tranent 7–0 East Kilbride
Formartine United 3–2 Clydebank
Brechin City 1–2 The Spartans
Jeanfield Swifts 6–0 Elgin City

190 | Cup Tied

The good things in life at Peterhead.

Curtains for this year's cup after the final at Hampden. Photographs by Daniel Gray

Huntly 1–4 Forfar Athletic (a.e.t.)
Pollok 5–2 Gala Fairydean Rovers
30 October 2023
CHAPTER 3 → Musselburgh Athletic 2–3 Clyde (a.e.t.)
Luncarty 0–1 Bo'ness United

THIRD ROUND
24 November 2023
CHAPTER 4 → Dunfermline Athletic 0–3 Raith Rovers
Clyde 2–0 Jeanfield Swifts
25 November 2023
Cumnock Juniors 0–3 Broomhil
Partick Thistle 3–0 Queen's Park
Greenock Morton 4–0 Bo'ness United
Annan Athletic 4–5 Dumbarton (a.e.t.)
Stranraer 0–1 Airdrieonians
Dunbar United 1–2 Alloa Athletic
Broxburn Athletic 2–2 Buckie Thistle (a.e.t.) (4–5 pens)
Hamilton Academical 0–2 Kelty Hearts
Brora Rangers 1–0 Pollok
Montrose 3–0 Edinburgh City
Falkirk 3–0 Formartine United
Stirling Albion 0–2 Cove Rangers
Inverness Caledonian Thistle 2–0 Cowdenbeath
CHAPTER 4 → Peterhead 1–2 Ayr United
Tranent 0–1 Forfar Athletic
Queen of the South 2–2 Dundee United (a.e.t.) (4–3 pens)
The Spartans 2–1 Arbroath
Albion Rovers 0–1 Bonnyrigg Rose

FOURTH ROUND
19 January 2024
Clyde 0–2 Aberdeen
20 January 2024
The Spartans 1–2 Heart of Midlothian
Ayr United 3–0 Kelty Hearts
Kilmarnock 2–0 Dundee
Greenock Morton 2–0 Montrose
Inverness Caledonian Thistle 4–0 Broomhill
St Mirren 1–0 Queen of the South
Bonnyrigg Rose 2–1 Falkirk
Livingston 2–1 Raith Rovers
Motherwell 3–1 Alloa Athletic
Ross County 0–3 Partick Thistle
CHAPTER 5 → Forfar Athletic 0–1 Hibernian
Airdrieonians 1–0 St Johnstone
Dumbarton 1–4 Rangers
21 January 2024
CHAPTER 5 → Celtic 5–0 Buckie Thistle
30 January 2024
Brora Rangers 1–3 Cove Rangers (a.e.t.)

FIFTH ROUND
9 February 2024
CHAPTER 6 → Greenock Morton 2–1 Motherwell
10 February 2024
Kilmarnock 2–0 Cove Rangers
Inverness Caledonian Thistle 1–3 Hibernian
CHAPTER 6 → Aberdeen 2–0 Bonnyrigg Rose

Partick Thistle 2–3 Livingston (a.e.t.)
Rangers 2–0 Ayr United
11 February 2024
St Mirren 0–2 Celtic
Airdrieonians 1–4 Heart of Midlothian

QUARTER-FINALS
9 March 2024
CHAPTER 7 → Aberdeen 3–1 Kilmarnock
10 March 2024
Celtic 4–2 Livingston
CHAPTER 7 → Hibernian 0–2 Rangers
11 March 2024
Greenock Morton 0–1 Heart of Midlothian

SEMI-FINALS
20 April 2024
CHAPTER 8 → Aberdeen 3–3 Celtic (a.e.t.) (5–6 pens)
21 April 2024
CHAPTER 8 → Rangers 2–0 Heart of Midlothian

FINAL
25 May 2024
CHAPTER 9 → Celtic 1–0 Rangers

The 2023/24 Scottish Cup marked the 150th anniversary of the tournament and was the 139th time the famous trophy had been competed for. 131 teams took part, starting on 12 August 2023 and ending at Hampden Park on 25 May 2024.

Cup Tied | 191

Daniel Gray is a writer and broadcaster, and the Editor of Nutmeg magazine. He is the author of several football books including *Saturday, 3pm* and *The Silence of the Stands*, shortlisted for the Sunday Times Football Book of the Year Award and longlisted for the William Hill Prize. Gray also writes on social history and travel, and his most recent work, *Food of the Cods: How Fish & Chips Made Britain* was shortlisted for Fortnum & Mason and Food Writers' Guild awards. He has written for most UK newspapers, presented history on television and regularly talked about football on local and national radio. He also presents the When Saturday Comes podcast.

Alan McCredie is a photographer, lecturer and film maker. A Perthshire lad lost to Edinburgh, he supports St Johnstone FC. He is the photographer/author of six previous books, including the Saltire-nominated *This is Scotland* with Daniel Gray, *My Scotland* with Val McDermid and *Scotland the Dreich*. His portrait and documentary work has appeared in a number of exhibitions over the years, and his epic 100 Weeks of Scotland project saw him take different images of this country in the two years leading up to the 2014 independence referendum. Alan lectures at Edinburgh College and lives in Leith. In their photo essays, he and Daniel are driven by a passion to find the perfect chip butty.

What is Nutmeg?
Published every three months, Nutmeg is the high-class home for quality articles about Scottish football's past, present and future. It offers opinion, reflection, interviews, insight, nostalgia, illustration and photography. It is a unique blend between 196 uniquely elegant pages.

Subscribe:
www.nutmegmagazine.co.uk
It's our game. In print.
Substack:
http://nutmegfootball.substack.com